WILL THE CHURCH GO THROUGH THE TRIBULATION?

Unless otherwise specified, all Scriptures are taken from the King James Version of the Holy Bible.

Will the Church Go Through the Tribulation?
© 2013, Southwest Radio Church of the Air

All rights reserved under International Copyright Law. No part of this book may be used or reproduced in any manner whatsoever without written permission of the publisher, except in the case of brief quotations in articles and reviews. For more information call or write:

Bible Belt Publishing
500 Beacon Dr., Oklahoma City, OK 73127
(800) 652-1144
www.swrc.com

Printed in the United States of America

ISBN 1-933641-52-5

WILL THE CHURCH GO THROUGH THE TRIBULATION?

NOAH W. HUTCHINGS ◆ BOB GLAZE
LARRY SPARGIMINO ◆ KENNETH HILL
DAVID SCHNITTGER ◆ DOUGLAS STAUFFER

Table of Contents

Introduction
by Noah Hutchings 7

The Church and the Tribulation in Genesis
by Bob Glaze 9

The Pre-Tribulational Rapture in the Book of Daniel?
by David Schnittger 17

The Tribulation Prophesied in the Four Gospels
by Larry Spargimino 32

The Tribulation Prophesied in Acts
by Noah Hutchings 46

The Tribulation Prophesied in the Pauline Epistles
by Douglas Stauffer 54

The Pre-Tribulational Rapture Prophesied in the General Epistles
by David Schnittger 79

The Tribulation Prophesied in the Book of Revelation
by Noah Hutchings 89

The Church After the Rapture
by Kenneth C. Hill 102

The Post-Tribulational World
by Larry Spargimino 123

Conclusion
by Noah Hutchings 143

Introduction

by Noah Hutchings

In this book, *Will the Church Go Through the Tribulation?*, several authors have considered separate but relative sections of both the Old and New Testaments, to see if the church (born-again Christians) will be in this coming time of famine, death, and sorrow.

The coming Tribulation will be the seventieth prophetic week of Daniel, a period of seven years that will witness the rebuilding of the temple in Jerusalem and the rise of a world dictator who will have the authority and power to demand that everyone in the world take his mark and worship him as God. Those who do not will be executed, as the Scriptures indicate that they will be beheaded.

Those who hold to a pre-tribulational view understand the Scriptures to mean all Christians will be taken up out of the world at the Rapture just before the Tribulation begins. Those who hold to a post-tribulational view believe the Scriptures teach that Christians will go through the Tribulation and will be persecuted and killed like everyone else. It is obvious that both views cannot be right, and this is what divides the fundamental and conservative Christians into two groups.

In this book, Dr. Larry Spargimino, Dr. Noah Hutchings, Dr. Bob Glaze, Dr. David Schnittger, Dr. Kenneth Hill, and Dr. Douglas Stauffer, all authors of books on biblical prophecy, consider different sections of the Bible to see, practically, if Christians will be subject to this most terrible time in world history.

The Church and the Tribulation in Genesis

by Bob Glaze

The question that is debated more and more as time goes on is, Will the church go through the Tribulation? The Tribulation period is to be defined as a specific seven-year period known as "Jacob's trouble," as described in Jeremiah 30:7. Will the church be removed prior to that judgment by what is called the Rapture?

The Rapture of the church, or saints, is to be defined as a time yet future wherein the Lord will return to remove His saints from the presence of wrath of the ungodly. The word *rapture* comes from 1 Thessalonians 4:17, "Then we which are alive and remain shall be **caught up** together with them in the clouds, to meet the Lord in the air: and so shall we ever be with the Lord"(emphasis mine). The original Greek word *harpazo* translates into the Latin word *raptus*, which transliterated produces the English word "rapture," meaning "snatched away" or "removed by force." If it can be shown that God's people are removed from the scene by natural or supernatural means before major judgments on the ungodly are enacted, then it proves that the church will not go through the Tribulation.

The future redemption of the saints of God and the final judgment of His enemies was determined in one verse of Scripture—Genesis 3:15: "And I will put enmity . . . between thy seed and her seed; it shall bruise thy head, and thou shalt bruise his heel." This prophecy was fulfilled at the cross with the crucifixion of Christ and His victory over death and the grave. Satan's fate was finalized, but his battle rages on in his attempt to overcome the curse placed upon him by his Victor.

This is not a battle of attrition, but one that is fulfilling God's plan of the ages. The date of the believers in Christ's removal at the Rapture is not ours to know, but until then the work of Christ continues. And, "The Lord knoweth how to deliver the godly out of temptations, and to reserve the unjust unto the day of judgment to be punished" (2 Peter 2:9). The "day of judgment" that Peter is referring to is still yet future and can only mean the Tribulation period. Since Scripture indicates that there is a future need for a righteous remnant to be removed, then there must be a reason, that being the Tribulation period.

One of the core principles taught throughout Scripture is the deliverance of the saints prior to God's wrath being unleashed upon the ungodly. The Old Testament saints experienced this deliverance on many occasions. The Christian is promised this in the greatest proof-text of a pre-tribulational Rapture in 1 Thessalonians 5:9: "For God hath not appointed us to wrath, but to obtain salvation by our Lord Jesus Christ."

When prior deliverance is taught, it precedes judgment. So, therefore, the Rapture or removal of the Christians, commonly called the church, must take place before the seven-year Tribulation period in order to preserve His remnant. This chronological order is taught throughout the Old Testament and establishes His method of saving a remnant. This chapter deals with a few of these instances.

Enoch

God created the earth and everything in it for one reason: to have communion with man. No other creature had the reason and ability to commune with Him: "And God said, Let us make man in our image, after our likeness: and let them have dominion over the fish of the sea, and over the fowl of the air, and over the cattle, and over all the earth, and over every creeping thing that creepeth upon the earth" (Genesis 1:26). It is reasonable to conclude that God intended for man to live forever, because death did not enter into the conversation until after the fall. Even though Cain killed his brother Abel in Genesis 4:8, "death" as a natural consequence of sin entered into the mix in Genesis 5:5: "And all the days that Adam lived were nine hundred and thirty years: and he died." In the faith chapter, Hebrews 11:4, the blood sacrifice is introduced as necessary beyond works: "By faith Abel offered unto God a more excellent sacrifice than Cain, by which he obtained witness that he was righteous, God testifying of his gifts . . ." (compare with Genesis 4:2–4).

The lineage of Adam continued in the following verses to include all of Adam's family until we come to verse 24: "And Enoch walked with God: and he was not; for God took him." He is the exception in this chapter of death. There is no other explanation other than he did not die. Why? The Hebrew word used here is the same as the word used for the translation of Elijah. He went straight to Heaven without seeing death. Again in Hebrews 11:5, we add faith to salvation with the words: "By faith Enoch was translated that he should not see death; and was not found, because God had translated him: for before his translation he had this testimony, that he pleased God." He was not rewarded for his works but rather for faith in his Creator, precluding any blind selection for salvation. Because of his existing faith, he was removed from the path of destruction.

Enoch is a picture of the believers that are alive at the Rapture and are taken before the coming judgment, the Tribulation period. This, many believe, establishes future removal of His remnant prior to judgment.

Noah and His Family

The Creator established the precedence concerning salvation of a remnant prior to the destruction of the many in Genesis 6. He chose Noah to provide a vehicle in which he, his family, and anyone else that would get on board could survive the coming catastrophe. According to Genesis 6, the entire earth had become corrupt, and violence was rampant so much that it grieved God that He had created man. We read in verse 6: "And it repented the LORD that he had made man on the earth, and it grieved him at his heart." Did the Lord make a mistake? No! Was He caught by surprise that man turned out the way he did? No! Although we may not understand why He used this plan to introduce Christ and the plan of salvation, it did show the need for a Saviour.

Before He destroyed the entire race of man He chose one man that met His qualifications for replenishing the earth after the flood, and that was Noah. In verse 8, we read: "But Noah found grace in the eyes of the Lord." Out of perhaps millions He found only one man, the absolute minimum to start over. When God gave him the blueprints to build the ark, little did Noah know that he was building the foreshadowing of the One that would ultimately be the Ark of Salvation. That Ark will deliver His saints before the impending doom of the Tribulation period.

The Lord prophesied the coming worldwide judgment in verse 3: "And the LORD said, My Spirit shall not always strive with man, for that he also is flesh: yet his days shall be an hundred and twenty years." The Lord not only told mankind that judgment was coming, but also told them when it was to come, at least the year, not the day or hour. Here the Lord set the future precedent of removal of a remnant prior to judgment when He told Noah to build an ark for him to escape the coming flood, as told in verse 17: "And, behold, I, even I, do bring a flood of waters upon the earth, to destroy all flesh, wherein is the breath of life, from under heaven; and every thing that is in the earth shall die." It is amazing to think that after one hundred years of preaching of the coming judgment that only eight people entered the ark.

After they entered the ark, God gave the masses another seven days of grace to change their minds. Here Noah is a type of Christ who was only able to save those that came to him by faith and entered into the ark. Christ is able only to save those that come to Him in faith. The eight that entered the ark were carried safely past the destruction of the world, as those that are raptured will be carried safely past the coming Tribulation period.

Again, "For God hath not appointed us to wrath, but to obtain salvation by our Lord Jesus Christ." For seven days they were given a grace period to enter into the ark, and so through seven years of the Tribulation period will men be given a chance to refuse the mark of the Beast and enter into "The Ark." "The Lord is not slack concerning his promise, as some men count slackness; but is longsuffering to us-ward, not willing that any should perish, but that all should come to repentance" (2 Peter 3:9).

Lot Delivered from Sodom

The biblical account of the destruction of Sodom and Gomorrah, as reported in Genesis 18–19, is built around one man and his life in a city apparently dominated by homosexuals. Sodomites are called homosexuals today because of social expedience. But their sin now is just as grievous to God as it was in Lot's day, as mentioned in Genesis 18:20: "And the LORD said, Because the cry of Sodom and Gomorrah is great, and because their sin is very grievous." The "cry" was most certainly that of Lot as he cried out for justice and deliverance.

The mention of Lot's life among the ungodly and the destruction of the two cities is a warning of future judgment in 2 Peter 2:6–8: "And turning the cities of Sodom and Gomorrha into ashes condemned them with an overthrow, making them an ensample unto those that after should live ungodly; And delivered just Lot, vexed with the filthy conversation of the wicked."

Since Sodom and Gomorrah are examples to others that follow the same sinful lifestyle, it is logical to believe that other cities of like lifestyles will meet with the same fate. Sodomy has permeated the entire globe and has become a blight to every country on earth, including even Israel. The cry of the Christian concerning this "very grievous" sin is being heard in Heaven and is not being ignored. This is possibly the core reason that the earth will be renovated by fire, as noted in 2 Peter 3:10: "But the day of the Lord will come as a thief in the night; in the which the heavens shall pass away with a great noise, and the elements shall melt with fervent heat, the earth also and the works that are therein shall be burned up."

The day of the Lord begins unexpectedly at the beginning of the Tribulation period, after the Rapture, and climaxes with the renovation (or destruction) of the earth at the end of the millennium. The conversation mentioned by Peter is not about their language, although it was most certainly abominable, but their practice of degradation of the vilest sense. Although the population of Sodom was not mentioned, there were not even ten righteous that could be found that were not afflicted with this spiritual disease. We know from reports that homosexuality is spreading like an airborne virus and may engulf the world at a time prior to the Rapture. It is possible that almost the entire population of the earth may be acting homosexuals just prior to the Tribulation and only the righteous will escape. It is therefore possible that the Antichrist will be a homosexual and the masses will willingly accept the mark of the Beast. In this way, those refusing to accept the mark may be identified.

The biblical historical account of Lot and the cities of Sodom and Gomorrah is a picture of the righteous being removed prior to the judgment of the ungodly. In Genesis 19:16 we find that Lot and his wife were forcefully removed by the angels before the event: "And while he lingered, the men laid hold upon his hand, and upon the hand of his wife, and upon the hand of his two daughters; the LORD being merciful unto him: and they brought him forth, and set him without the city." As previously noted, one of the meanings of the English word "rapture" means to be taken away by force. The angel took them by force. Another picture is found in verse 22 of the same chapter: "Haste thee, escape thither; for I cannot do any thing till thou be come thither. Therefore the name of the city was called Zoar."

Joseph: A Type of Christ

Joseph was a type of Christ in many ways, but here we are only interested in the scenarios that pertained to the Rapture and "Jacob's trouble." In Genesis 41:45 we read that Joseph, like Christ, took a gentile bride before a seven-year period that plunged the entire world into famine: "And Pharaoh called Joseph's name Zaphnath-paaneah; and he gave him to wife Asenath the daughter of Poti-pherah priest of On. . . ." During the famine, all the world cried to Joseph for salvation.

The prophecy of Mark 13:8 gives us the same picture: ". . . and there shall be famines and troubles. . . ." While there are certainly differences in Joseph's life compared to the life of Jesus, the scenarios are remarkably similar. His brothers that sold him into slavery were made to recognize their sin of rejection and were restored to his favor, as will be Israel after the seven-year Tribulation period.

In that period many turned to Joseph for help, as will Israel turn to Jesus as the "Lord" that they rejected as the supplier of all their needs. At the Rapture and before the Tribulation period, Jesus will take His gentile bride prior to the seven years of spiritual famine. During that period, we will experience the judgment seat and the marriage supper of the Lamb. After the seven-year Tribulation period, we as His bride rule and reign with Him for a thousand years.

There are other portions of Scripture in the Old Testament that prove that God's people are always removed before the destruction of the ungodly. These will be brought out in additional chapters of this book.

The Pre-Tribulational Rapture in the Book of Daniel?

by David Schnittger

In this chapter we will continue to answer the question, Will the church go through the Tribulation? We will be exploring the great prophetic Book of Daniel to see if there is any clue as to the church's presence in the Tribulation. Daniel is the premier Old Testament book when it comes to prophecy. It speaks of the rise and character of the Antichrist and of the peace treaty that he will execute with Israel that will begin the Tribulation. It reveals much about the kingdom of the Antichrist that will dominate the Tribulation period. It speaks of the preservation of a remnant of Israel during the Tribulation, as well as the resurrection of Israel's dead that will take place after the Tribulation. Indeed, the Book of Daniel is the Old Testament corollary to the Book of Revelation as it relates to end-time prophecy.

Is the Church in Daniel?

At the outset, it is important to be reminded of what the Apostle Paul said about the disclosure of truth regarding the church in this present dispensation of grace. We read in Ephesians 3:1–6:

> For this cause I Paul, the prisoner of Jesus Christ for you Gentiles, If ye have heard of the dispensation of the grace of God which is given me to you-ward: How that by revelation he made known unto me the mystery. . . . Which in other ages was not made known unto the sons of men, as it is now revealed unto his holy apostles and prophets by the Spirit; That the Gentiles should be fellowheirs, and of the same body, and partakers of his promise in Christ by the gospel.

Paul is saying that the church, which is made up of Jews and gentiles brought together in absolute spiritual equality (Ephesians 2:15), did not exist under the old covenant. Not only that, but Paul is saying that information about the church was not revealed in the Old Testament. It was a "mystery" or secret not revealed in previous times, such as the Old Testament or the gospels. It is the failure to recognize the "mystery" character of the church that leads to such fallacies as the amillennial view which interprets Daniel's seventieth week (Daniel 9:24–27) as past and as having its fulfillment (or terminus) at the death of Christ. Amillennialists employ an allegorical interpretive approach to Daniel's seventy-weeks prophecy to prove the political and spiritual program for the Jewish people ended with the first advent of Christ and has been replaced by the church. In other words, according to amillennialists, the millennium is taking place during the church age, as the world is currently being ruled by Christ through the agency of the church. There is no future for the nation Israel according to this view.

However, if we take Paul's revelation in Ephesians 3 seriously, we will not expect to find any information about the church in the

Book of Daniel. The Book of Daniel relates to historical information about a remnant of Judah in captivity (606–536 B.C.) as well as the future of Israel during the Tribulation period and beyond.

We should, therefore, not expect Daniel to deal with issues such as the Rapture of the church, since the church is not revealed in the book. Having said that, we are now free to explore some of the wonderful prophecies of the Book of Daniel and should expect that Daniel will confirm that the church will not be present during the time of Jacob's (Israel's) trouble (Jeremiah 30:7). In effect, our argument is based on omission. The church is simply not mentioned in the Book of Daniel, so we would expect that the church will not be present when the tribulational events Daniel describes takes place. This will only be a quick survey of the prophetic highlights of Daniel. For a more detailed study of the book, I recommend *Daniel the Prophet* by Noah Hutchings (Bible Belt Publishing, 2011).

The Image of Daniel 2

Let's begin by considering the prophecy of four kingdoms in Daniel 2:31–45. King Nebuchadnezzar's dream of an image depicted the kingdoms of Babylon (605–539 B.C.), Medo-Persia (538–333 B.C.), Greece (333–160 B.C.), Rome (160 B.C.–A.D. 500), the Roman colonial system to A.D. 1945, and the Restored Federated Rome to the second coming of Jesus Christ.

Notice Daniel's description of the fourth kingdom (Daniel 2:40–43):

> And the fourth kingdom shall be strong as iron: forasmuch as iron breaketh in pieces and subdueth all things: and as iron that breaketh all these, shall it break in pieces and bruise. And whereas thou

sawest the feet and toes, part of potters' clay, and part of iron, the kingdom shall be divided; but there shall be in it of the strength of the iron, forasmuch as thou sawest the iron mixed with miry clay. And as the toes of the feet were part of iron, and part of clay, so the kingdom shall be partly strong, and partly broken. And whereas thou sawest iron mixed with miry clay, they shall mingle themselves with the seed of men: but they shall not cleave one to another, even as iron is not mixed with clay.

This fourth kingdom, the Roman Empire, began to break up in A.D. 476 but endured in some form until A.D. 963 when its dissolution became complete. Even so, as Daniel foretold, Rome continued to rule the world in its broken state. Each chunk of iron in the legs of the image became an empire: the Spanish Empire, the British Empire, the Dutch Empire, the Italian Empire, the Belgian Empire, the French Empire, etc.

Also, according to Daniel's prophecy, these competing empires would "mingle themselves with the seed of men" (Daniel 2:43). In other words, they would jostle against one another and fight one another.

History records the literal fulfillment of this part of the prophecy: French-English wars, Spanish-English wars, the Napoleonic wars, and both World War I and World War II were started by European powers that were once integral parts of the Old Roman Empire.

Almost immediately after World War II, the Roman colonial system began to break up. The colonies of France, England, Germany, Italy, Holland, Belgium, etc., gained their independence. All that remains of these chunks of the Old Roman Empire are the nations of the British Commonwealth, such as Canada, Australia, and New Zealand.

Daniel refers to the "toes" of this Roman Empire in Daniel 2:42.

These ten toes represent a kingdom in the very extremity of the age. Even though the kingdom would break into pieces and never cleave together again, the pieces themselves are still referred to as a kingdom. Even in the toes we find the iron and the clay mixed together. We refer to this kingdom in the end of the age as the Revived Roman Empire, commonly known as the European Union.

Notice what the prophet Daniel says will eventually follow the formation of this union:

> And in the days of these kings shall the God of heaven set up a kingdom, which shall never be destroyed: and the kingdom shall not be left to other people, but it shall break in pieces and consume all these kingdoms, and it shall stand for ever. Forasmuch as thou sawest that the stone was cut out of the mountain without hands, and that it brake in pieces the iron, the brass, the clay, the silver, and the gold; the great God hath made known to the king what shall come to pass hereafter: and the dream is certain, and the interpretation thereof sure. —Daniel 2:44–45

Daniel tells us that in the days of the kings of the ten-nation kingdom that will rise up out of the Roman Empire at the end of the gentile age, God will send Jesus Christ back. He is depicted as a rock appearing out of the sky to strike the gentile image on its feet, and the entire monstrosity crumbles into dust and is blown away. But the rock becomes a huge mountain and fills the whole earth.

Notice first that this stone which strikes the image is cut out of a mountain without hands. In other words, man had nothing to do with it. It is extraterrestrial in origin. This would certainly apply to Jesus Christ, who was born without the agent of a human father. Such a stone was prophesied in Isaiah 28:16: "Therefore thus saith the Lord

GOD, Behold, I lay in Zion for a foundation a stone, a tried stone, a precious corner stone, a sure foundation: he that believeth shall not make haste."

This rock is identified in 1 Corinthians 10:4: "And did all drink the same spiritual drink: for they drank of that spiritual Rock that followed them: and that Rock was Christ." Then we read in Matthew 21:42, 44: "Jesus saith unto them, Did ye never read in the scriptures, The stone which the builders rejected, the same is become the head of the corner: this is the Lord's doing, and it is marvellous in our eyes? . . . And whosoever shall fall on this stone shall be broken: but on whomsoever it shall fall, it will grind him to powder."

Can there be any doubt that the rock which smote the image in the dream of Nebuchadnezzar, and literally ground it to powder, is none other than Jesus Christ? But let us not suppose that Jesus Christ is coming back to destroy the world. We read in Daniel 2:44 that He is coming back to set up His own kingdom—a kingdom that will never be possessed or conquered by another, and a kingdom that will never pass away. We read about that kingdom in Revelation 11:15: ". . . The kingdoms of this world are become the kingdoms of our Lord, and of his Christ; and he shall reign for ever and ever."

The Beasts of Chapter Seven

Let's move now to Daniel's prophecy in chapter seven. Here Daniel refers to the gentile kingdoms as "beasts." They are described in Daniel 7:3–7:

> And four great beasts came up from the sea, diverse one from another. The first was like a lion, and had eagle's wings: I beheld till the wings thereof were plucked, and it was lifted up from the

earth, and made stand upon the feet as a man, and a man's heart was given to it. And behold another beast, a second, like to a bear, and it raised up itself on one side, and it had three ribs in the mouth of it between the teeth of it: and they said thus unto it, Arise, devour much flesh. After this I beheld, and lo another, like a leopard, which had upon the back of it four wings of a fowl; the beast had also four heads; and dominion was given to it. After this I saw in the night visions, and behold a fourth beast, dreadful and terrible, and strong exceedingly; and it had great iron teeth: it devoured and brake in pieces, and stamped the residue with the feet of it: and it was diverse from all the beasts that were before it; and it had ten horns.

The use of the expression "four great beasts" in this passage is very instructive. God looks upon nations, and leaders of nations who are completely humanistic, as beastlike in thought and deed. We read in Revelation 13 that the Antichrist, the last world ruler, is called a beast. Nations that become empires always have predatory beasts as emblems. Nations become empires by eating up other nations.

In this vision, we can determine that four great world powers will be stirred up by the powers of Satan to rise up in the Mediterranean area. The generally accepted interpretation of Daniel's vision concerning the four beasts corresponds to the four divisions of the image which Nebuchadnezzar saw in a dream. The beast like a lion with eagle's wings is Babylon; the bear with three ribs in his mouth is Medo-Persia; the beast like a leopard with four wings of a fowl is Greece; and the last beast, which was too dreadful and terrible for Daniel to describe, is Rome. Noah Hutchings, in his book *Daniel the Prophet*, intriguingly suggests that the four beasts are modern empires: lion (England), eagle (United States), bear (Russia), leopard (Africa). Whatever the identification of these four beasts, it is instructive to note the end of these kingdoms in Daniel 7:19–22:

> Then I would know the truth of the fourth beast, which was diverse from all the others, exceeding dreadful, whose teeth were of iron, and his nails of brass; which devoured, brake in pieces, and stamped the residue with his feet; And of the ten horns that were in his head, and of the other which came up, and before whom three fell; even of that horn that had eyes, and a mouth that spake very great things, whose look was more stout than his fellows. I beheld, and the same horn made war with the saints, and prevailed against them; Until the Ancient of days came, and judgment was given to the saints of the most High; and the time came that the saints possessed the kingdom.

The fourth beast is the Antichrist. Many believe that the ten horns in his head refer to the ten regions that will make up the "new world order" of the Antichrist. It is important to note that, in both the image of Daniel 2 and the beasts of Daniel 7, the church and the Rapture are nowhere mentioned.

The Description of the Antichrist

Daniel 8 continues the description of the Antichrist. In Daniel 8:9–14 he is referred to as "the little horn":

> And out of one of them came forth a little horn, which waxed exceeding great, toward the south, and toward the east, and toward the pleasant land. And it waxed great, even to the host of heaven; and it cast down some of the host and of the stars to the ground, and stamped upon them. Yea, he magnified himself even to the

prince of the host, and by him the daily sacrifice was taken away, and the place of his sanctuary was cast down. And a host was given him against the daily sacrifice by reason of transgression, and it cast down the truth to the ground; and it practised, and prospered. Then I heard one saint speaking, and another saint said unto *that certain saint which spake, How long shall be the vision concerning the daily sacrifice,* and the transgression of desolation, to give both the sanctuary and the host to be trodden under foot? And he said unto me, Unto two thousand and three hundred days; then shall the sanctuary be cleansed.

There is some division among Bible expositors as to the identity of the little horn. Many believe that this prophecy was fulfilled when Antiochus Epiphanes, the governor of Syria, took Jerusalem and defiled the temple by offering a sow upon the altar (167 B.C.). There is a great similarity between the little horn of chapter eight and Antiochus Epiphanes. Martin Luther said: "This chapter in Daniel refers to both Antiochus and Antichrist." Most Bible scholars concur with Luther's view: the prophecy was fulfilled in type in Antiochus, but the real little horn will be the Antichrist. In other words, the little horn of chapter eight that grew up out of one of the four notable horns is the same little horn of chapter seven who comes up in the middle of the ten horns on the head of the terrible beast.

The Antichrist is also referred to in chapter eight as "a king of fierce countenance":

> And in the latter time of their kingdom, when the transgressors are come to the full, *a king of fierce countenance,* and understanding dark sentences, shall stand up. And his power shall be mighty, but not by his own power: and he shall destroy wonderfully, and shall prosper, and practise, and shall destroy the mighty and the holy

people. And through his policy also he shall cause craft to prosper in his hand; and he shall magnify himself in his heart, and by peace shall destroy many: he shall also stand up against the Prince of princes; but he shall be broken without hand. —Daniel 8:23–25

We are informed in this chapter that the Antichrist would be mighty, but not by his power. This implies that his power is satanic. He would march southward across the Mediterranean and take North Africa, and then turn eastward toward Jerusalem. He would claim to be a man of peace, and by peace destroy many. He would also be a man of industry and crafts—he will cause a great business boom in the world, and especially within his own ten-nation kingdom, which most believe will be the Revived Roman Empire, known today as the European Union.

Daniel's Seventieth Week

As we move into chapter nine of the book of Daniel, we are attracted to verses 24–27, known as the prophecy of Daniel's seventieth week:

Seventy weeks are determined upon thy people and upon thy holy city, to finish the transgression, and to make an end of sins, and to make reconciliation for iniquity, and to bring in everlasting righteousness, and to seal up the vision and prophecy, and to anoint the most Holy. Know therefore and understand, that from the going forth of the commandment to restore and to build Jerusalem unto the Messiah the Prince shall be seven weeks, and threescore and two weeks: the street shall be built again, and the wall, even in troublous times. And after threescore and two weeks shall Messiah be cut off, but not for himself: and the people of the prince that shall come shall destroy the city and the sanctuary; and the end thereof shall be with a flood, and unto the end of the war desolations are determined. And he shall confirm the covenant with many for one week: and in the midst of the week he shall cause the sacrifice and the oblation to cease, and for the overspreading of abominations he shall make it desolate, even until the consummation, and that determined shall be poured upon the desolate.

Notice that this prophecy regarding seventy weeks (490 years) involves six things:

1. Finish the transgression
2. Make an end of sin
3. Make reconciliation for iniquity
4. Bring in everlasting righteousness
5. Seal up the vision and prophecy
6. Anoint the most Holy

In considering the meaning of each of the six things which Gabriel prophesied, let us keep in mind that, according to verse 24, they concern Israel as a race, the holy city Jerusalem, the land of Palestine, and the temple. The prophecy is Jewish from beginning to end. Gentiles are not even referred to, and the church age is completely hidden from view. Without going into the complexities of this prophecy, rest assured that all six of the things which Daniel prayed for will be fulfilled when Israel receives the Messiah at the end of the Tribulation. The hope of those things promised by God in the covenants lay in a Saviour, a Redeemer, a Deliverer, the One whom the New Testament reveals as the Lord Jesus Christ. The Messiah will come to Israel at the end of the seventy prophetic weeks, but first He must be cut off for the sins of the world.

More Insights Regarding the Antichrist

The eleventh chapter of Daniel gives us further insights regarding the Antichrist. He is referred to in Daniel 11:3–4 as a "mighty king":

> And a *mighty king* shall stand up, that shall rule with great dominion, and do according to his will. And when he shall stand up, his kingdom shall be broken, and shall be divided toward the four winds of heaven; and not to his posterity, nor according to his dominion which he ruled: for his kingdom shall be plucked up, even for others beside those.

The Antichrist is also referred to as the "king of the north" in Daniel 11:15–17, 36–45. One interesting insight regarding his ethnicity and sexual preference is found in Daniel 11:36–37:

> And the king shall do according to his will; and he shall exalt himself, and magnify himself above every god, and shall speak marvellous things against the God of gods, and shall prosper till the indignation be accomplished: for that that is determined shall be done. Neither shall he regard the God of his fathers, nor the desire of women, nor regard any god: for he shall magnify himself above all.

There are many Bible scholars who contend that the Antichrist will be a Jew because of the statement that he will not regard the God of his fathers, meaning father Abraham, father Isaac, and father Jacob. Also, it is reasoned that in order for the Jews to accept the Antichrist as messiah and accept his confirmation of the covenant, he would have to be one of their own people who had credentials indicating that he was of the lineage of David.

Notice also that he will not "... regard ... the desire of women." By the time Antichrist appears, homosexuals may be considered to be more normal than heterosexuals. It almost appears to be that way today, as our society continues to degenerate. Therefore, the prophecy that the Antichrist will not regard the "desire of women" could simply mean that he will be a homosexual. By the way, truth be told, that is the case with most world leaders today! For example, the meeting of male world leaders at the Bohemian Grove in Monte Rio, California, for two weeks each summer is accompanied by the importation of homosexual prostitutes to "service" these leaders.

The Resurrection of Israel's Dead

Let's move on to the twelfth and final chapter of the Book of Daniel. In Daniel 12:1–2 we read of a future resurrection:

> And at that time shall Michael stand up, the great prince which standeth for the children of thy people: and there shall be a time of trouble, such as never was since there was a nation even to that same time: and at that time thy people shall be delivered, every one that shall be found written in the book. And many of them that sleep in the dust of the earth shall awake, some to everlasting life, and some to shame and everlasting contempt.

This unprecedented time of trouble that Daniel is referring to is the last half of the Tribulation period, known as "the Great Tribulation" (Matthew 24:21), which will follow the abomination of desolation (Daniel 9:27; 12:11; Matthew 24:15) when the Antichrist proclaims himself to be god in the temple at Jerusalem (2 Thessalonians 2:4).

At the end of the Great Tribulation there will be a resurrection, some to everlasting life, and some to shame and contempt. Who are those who will be resurrected to eternal life? It will be "thy people" Israel, as they are the subject of Daniel 12:1. The resurrection of the church is not in view here, because the Rapture of the church will have already occurred. There is no evidence that the church will go through the Tribulation in the Book of Daniel. Every saved person of the dispensation of grace will be caught up to be with the Lord before the Tribulation begins (1 Thessalonians 4:13–18). Daniel was not concerned about the gentiles; he was concerned only about his people, Israel. Daniel 12:2 in no way teaches a general resurrection. Some of Israel will be raised to everlasting life, and some of Israel will be raised to everlasting shame.

Summary

The Book of Daniel is a wonderful book of history and prophecy. It tells the dual story of God's faithfulness to Daniel and his three Hebrew friends during a long period of captivity, when the future of Judah and Israel looked dim. It also tells the story of God's faithfulness to Israel, despite the corruptions of future oppressive empires, culminating in the empire of the Antichrist that comes into full development during the Tribulation, the time of Jacob's trouble (Jeremiah 30:7). However, at the end of that period is promised the preservation of a remnant, the return of Israel's Messiah, the Lord Jesus Christ, the resurrection of Israel's faithful, and the establishment of the Messiah's kingdom with Israel at its center. This is the hope of Israel that is presented in the Book of Daniel!

As wonderful as that story is, the church is not in that story. The church occupies that still indeterminate period of time between the sixty-ninth and seventieth weeks of Daniel's prophecy. That "great parenthesis" is the church age, the dispensation of grace, born after the ascension of Christ and promoted to glory at the Rapture, prior to the commencement of Daniel's seventieth week, when God again returns His redemptive focus to the nation Israel. God has a wonderful plan for Israel, and He has a wonderful plan for the church. Let us not intermingle the two. We have seen God's wonderful plan for Israel in the Book of Daniel. In subsequent chapters we will examine God's wonderful plan for the church!

The Tribulation Prophesied in the Four Gospels

by Larry Spargimino

The Bible speaks of times of suffering for believers. Every believer will go through challenging times of tribulation. The Apostle Paul and Barnabas retraced their steps on their first missionary journey and sought to remind the new believers what they would face. Acts 14:22 reports that they confirmed "the souls of the disciples, and exhorting them to continue in the faith, and that we must through much *tribulation* enter into the kingdom of God."

However, there is also a period of time in the future that will reveal intense suffering and tribulation for God's people. The focus of this time of trouble would be Israel. "Alas! for that day is great," we read in Jeremiah 30:7, "so that none is like it: it is even the time of Jacob's trouble; but he shall be saved out of it."

Passages like this abound in both the Old and New Testaments, and especially in the gospels. Jeremiah is here speaking of a time period—"the time of Jacob's trouble." If the prophet had written "this day," we would likely conclude that his reference is only to the day of the Babylonian invasions of Jerusalem. However, the Spirit of inspiration has led Jeremiah to write "for [in] *that day,*" in some day other than the present day, perhaps in some future day.

It is important that the student of the prophetic Scriptures look closely at the details, and it is amazing how one detail, once understood, opens the eyes to another equally significant one. Jeremiah 30:4 speaks about both Israel and Judah, at least suggesting that both are reunited at some future time. Verses 8–9 speak about a restored theocratic government under a Davidic ruler, and a time of irreversible peace.

Other Old Testament scriptures provide additional insights into this "time of Jacob's trouble," such as Zechariah 13:8–9: "And it shall come to pass, that in all the land, saith the LORD, *two parts therein shall be cut off and die;* but the third shall be left therein. And *I will bring the third part through the fire, and will refine them as silver is refined,* and will try them as gold is tried: they shall call on my name, and I will hear them: I will say, It is my people: and they shall say, The LORD is my God."

There are many other Old Testament scriptures that speak of this future time of trouble for Israel. But what happens to this prophetic truth in the gospels? Is it eclipsed, or modified? What did the Lord Jesus Christ say about it?

Jesus on the Tribulation

Most people, even those who are not Christian, associate Jesus with love, forgiveness, and grace. And, indeed, the association is correct. But Jesus said much more. He spoke frankly about the end times.

While the most extensive biblical treatment of the Tribulation period in the New Testament is found in Revelation 6–19, there is also much in the gospels that parallels this section of Revelation. Matthew 24–25, Mark 13, and Luke 17 and 21 all record the words of Jesus dealing with this future period of "Jacob's trouble." According to the words of Jesus, the sufferings during the Tribulation will be intense, and will include both human conflict and natural disasters of cataclysmic proportions.

Because Jesus ministered in human flesh at the end of the Old Testament era and before the establishment of the church age, He sounded, in many respects, like a Hebrew prophet. "Woe unto thee, Chorazin! woe unto thee, Bethsaida! for if the mighty works, which were done in you, had been done in Tyre and Sidon, they would have repented long ago in sackcloth and ashes" (Matthew 11:21).

Jesus was presenting Himself as Messiah to Israel. Chorazin and Bethsaida were in the vicinity of Capernaum, near the northern shore of the Sea of Galilee. His great Galilean ministry was pervaded with miracles. Jesus was presenting Himself to Israel as her Messiah. Would they accept Him, or reject Him? In Jesus' teachings on the Tribulation, He explains what will happen to Israel as a result of her rejection of His messiahship.

With these thoughts in mind, let's proceed to delve into our topic, "The Tribulation Prophesied in the Gospels."

The Olivet Discourse

The most extensive teaching from Jesus on the end times is found in what has been known as the Olivet Discourse, so named because it was teaching given from the Mount of Olives. In Matthew 24:1–3 we read:

> And Jesus went out, and departed from the temple: and his disciples came to him for to shew him the buildings of the temple. And Jesus said unto them, See ye not all these things? verily I say unto you, There shall not be left here one stone upon another, that shall not be thrown down. And as he sat upon the mount of Olives, the

disciples came unto him privately, saying, Tell us, when shall these things be? and what shall be the sign of thy coming, and of the end of the world? (see also Mark 13:1–27; Luke 21:5–28)

The Olivet Discourse is clearly addressed to Israel, not to the church. This should not be surprising since the church age is a mystery later revealed through the Apostle Paul (Ephesians 3:1–6). The discourse is preceded by Jesus' heartfelt lamentation over Jerusalem (Matthew 23:37–39). The city and people had been given many opportunities at reconciliation with God, but they refused God's invitation:

O Jerusalem, Jerusalem, thou that killest the prophets, and stonest them which are sent unto thee, how often would I have gathered thy children together, even as a hen gathereth her chickens under her wings, and ye would not! Behold, your house is left unto you desolate. (vss. 37–38)

Though Israel has rejected her King, the Lord Jesus Christ still has a love for His people. The words "your house is left unto you desolate" is speaking about the destruction of the Jewish temple (Matthew 24:1–2).

When His disciples came to Him, Jesus answered their question about the temple and said: "See ye not all these things? verily I say unto you, There shall not be left here one stone upon another, that shall not be thrown down."

Jesus was referring to Herod's temple. It was a magnificent edifice built by Herod to ingratiate himself to the Jewish people. First century Jews would often comment that if you have never seen Herod's edifice, you have never seen a beautiful building. Not only was it elaborate and ornate, it was huge and very impressive. The temple was the pride of Jerusalem. The disciples must have received

Jesus' dire prediction with deep sorrow. They saw it as an event of apocalyptic proportions, hence their question in Matthew 24:3: "When shall these things be? and what shall be the sign of thy coming, and of the end of the world?"

"When shall these things be?" is a question regarding our Lord's statement that "there shall not be left here one stone upon another." The immediate reference would be the destruction of the Jewish temple in A.D. 70. Evidently, in the minds of the disciples this would happen at the time of Jesus "coming, and of the end of the world." The original-language word translated "world" is not *kosmos*, as in the phrase, "Love not the *world*, neither the things that are in the *world* . . ." (1 John 2:15), but rather *aion*, meaning "age," a period of time, as in the phrase "in the present age." The disciples were not asking about the end of the planet earth, for there will be ". . . new heavens and a new earth, wherein dwelleth righteousness" (2 Peter 3:13), but they were asking about the end of the present age of suffering, confusion, and domination by the Romans.

Evidently, the disciples thought that the destruction of the temple, the coming of the Lord, and the end of the age would all occur at the same time. They were partly correct in this estimation. The coming of the Lord would begin the kingdom age of Israel's glory, prophesied by the Hebrew prophets. However, they were wrong in tying in the impending destruction of the temple with the coming of the Lord and the kingdom age. Nor did they anticipate the church age, for such is declared to have been a mystery, hidden before the time it was revealed through the Apostle Paul (Ephesians 3:1–6).

Many Bible scholars, though not all, believe that while the disciples conjoined these three events, Christ did not. Matthew (chapter 24) and Mark (chapter 13) do not deal with the A.D. 70 destruction of Jerusalem in their presentation of the Olivet Discourse. Both of these evangelists focus on the future Tribulation period leading up to the establishment of the kingdom with the return of Israel's Messiah, Jesus Christ. Only in Luke's presentation is there material dealing with the Roman invasions (21:20–24). Of course, Luke also deals with the future Tribulation and the return of Jesus Christ (21:25–36). Matthew and Mark exclusively focus on answering the question, "What shall be the sign of thy coming, and of the end of the world?"

The question may be raised, How do we know that Luke 21:20–24 is dealing with the Roman invasion of Jerusalem in the first century A.D.? The answer would seem to lie in verse 24: "And they shall fall by the edge of the sword, and shall be led away captive into all nations: and Jerusalem shall be trodden down of the Gentiles, until the times of the Gentiles be fulfilled." The future Tribulation period is not followed by "the times of the Gentiles," a phrase indicating the current domination of Jerusalem by gentile forces, but rather by the kingdom age of Israel's glory. In Luke, Jesus is speaking about the trodding down of Jerusalem during a period of intense persecution by the gentiles. This could only be a reference to the humiliation of Jerusalem in the first century, and in the following centuries.

Jesus and the "Taking Away"

In Matthew 24:38–41 Jesus says:

> For as in the days that were before the flood they were eating and drinking, marrying and giving in marriage, until the day that Noe entered into the ark, And knew not until the flood came, and took them all away; so shall also the coming of the Son of man be. Then shall two be in the field; the one shall be taken, and the other left. Two women shall be grinding at the mill; the one shall be taken, and the other left.

The Bible says "the flood came, and took them all away." This was a taking away to their doom. This certainly cannot be the Rapture, for in the Rapture the taking away is a taking to Heaven, not a taking to death by drowning. It is, therefore, doubtful if this is the Rapture spoken of in 1 Thessalonians 4 and 1 Corinthians 15.

The questions of the disciples that Jesus answered were Israel-oriented (Matthew 24:1–2). Verse 15 is speaking about "the abomination of desolation." It has everything to do with the temple, which is Jewish, and it is the fulfillment of prophecy dealing with Israel (Daniel 9:27; cf. also Matthew 24:20, "sabbath day"). Believers during this period of Tribulation are to look for signs (Matthew 24:15), but church age Christians are directed to look for the Lord (Titus 2:13). The prophesied Tribulation in the gospels pertains to Israel, and what Israel will experience. It does not provide instruction for the church.

Even if nothing else is said in this study about the focus of the Olivet Discourse, it is clear that it is focused on Israel. Yet, there are several other considerations that reinforce this Jewish focus:

1. The Olivet Discourse grew out of questions regarding the Jewish temple (Matthew 24:2).
2. The disciples asked about Jesus' return at the end of the age. Since the church age was still a mystery, their question was not about Jesus' return for the church, but about His return for Israel, and attendant events.
3. Though Jesus does speak about the worldwide effects of the Tribulation, when He speaks about a specific area it is Judah (vs. 16).
4. He references a major Jewish institution, the Sabbath (vs. 20).
5. In His answer to His disciples, Jesus refers to Daniel the prophet (vs. 15) who prophesied about the Jewish people and the city of

Jerusalem (Daniel 9:24ff).
6. Jesus makes reference to "the gospel of the kingdom"—Israel's hope for the kingdom age (vs. 13). It is the "gospel" John preached (Matthew 3:2), the "gospel" Christ preached (4:12–17), the same gospel the disciples preached (10:7). The word "gospel" means "good news." "The gospel of the kingdom" is God's good news for Israel regarding Israel's glorification in the end times.

More than any of the other gospels, Matthew's is more closely connected with Israel and the Hebrew scriptures both in their theme and emphasis than the other gospels. There are numerous references to the Son of David (1:1, 20; 9:27; 12:23; 15:22; 20:30–31, et al), to the Mosaic Law (5:17–19, 21, 27, 31, 33, 38, 43; 7:12; 11:13, et al), and to the "holy city" and the "holy place" (4:5; 24:15; 27:53).

"The Beginning of Sorrows" and Beyond

In Matthew 24:7–8 Jesus speaks of nation rising "against nation, and kingdom against kingdom: and there shall be famines, and pestilences, and earthquakes, in divers places. All these are the beginning of sorrows." Then later in the chapter Jesus becomes specific: "For *then* shall be great tribulation, such as was not since the beginning of the world to this time, no, nor ever shall be." Some commentators say this is just allegorical language and try to find some poetic expressions in Scripture that have the idea of "such as was not since the beginning of the world . . . nor ever shall be" simply indicating a general time of suffering. However, in context, and especially in view of what follows, we can conclude that this is speaking about extreme end-time conditions that have never occurred before, nor will ever occur again.

The phrase "the beginning of sorrows" is suggestive of the beginning of the Tribulation period; but the words, "For *then* shall be *great* tribulation" seems to refer to the second part of the Tribulation period, known as the "Great Tribulation," which follows the revealing of the "abomination of desolation" of verse 15.

The question is often asked, Will anyone survive this horrible period of suffering and woe on the earth? Jesus says, Yes. In Matthew 24:22 He says: "And except those days should be shortened, there should no flesh be saved: but for the elect's sake those days shall be shortened."

The whole Tribulation period is seven years in duration. Does this mean that God will make it shorter than seven years? No; what the text most likely means is that the Tribulation period has a definite end. The period was shortened in the mind of God before it was ever revealed. If it were longer than seven years "there should no flesh be saved."

The Extent of the Tribulation Prophesied in the Gospels

Some commentators believe that the Tribulation has already occurred and its effects were local and limited to the area of Jerusalem. We believe that the Tribulation is yet future, and that Jesus teaches its universal extent.

In Luke 21:26 Jesus says that it will be a time when "men's hearts failing them for fear, and for looking after those things which are coming on the earth [*oikumene*]: for the powers of heaven shall be shaken." *Oikumene* refers to the whole inhabited world, the world made up of many peoples and tongues. It is contrasted with "Jerusalem" and "Judea" (vss. 20–21).

There are other considerations that show the Tribulation

prophesied by Jesus will affect the whole world. Jesus said, "And except those days should be shortened, there should *no flesh* be saved . . ." (Matthew 24:22).

The words "no flesh" are broad in extent. For example, in Romans 3:20 we read: "Therefore by the deeds of the law there shall *no flesh* be justified in his sight. . . ." Does the apostle mean, "No flesh in Jerusalem and Judea will be justified by keeping the Law, but everyone else will be justified by keeping the Law"?

First Corinthians 1:29 is similar: "That *no flesh* should glory in his presence." Does this mean that "no one living in Jerusalem and Judea in the first century should glory in God's presence, but that everyone else should do so"?

Hence, we can conclude that in the Olivet Discourse Jesus is speaking about a time of tribulation affecting both the earth and the heavens.

The Time of the Fulfillment of the Tribulation Prophesied in the Gospels

When are the prophecies of the Olivet Discourse fulfilled? Preterists generally hold to some kind of a first century fulfillment, whereas futurists believe that these prophecies will be fulfilled in the future.

In Matthew 24:22 there is another key that gives away much regarding the Tribulation: "And except those days should be shortened, there should no flesh be saved: *but for the elect's sake those days shall be shortened."* Jesus is giving a promise. The elect will be saved. He loves them, and has considered them.

Preterists believe that the Olivet Discourse was fulfilled in A.D. 70. But what happened in A.D. 70? How many were saved? How many were delivered? A.D. 70 was not about deliverance but about disaster. But that's not the complete meaning and intent of the Olivet

Discourse. It doesn't speak of Israel's final doom, but rather about Israel's final deliverance.

In Matthew 24:15–21 Jesus speaks about great trouble for Israel. He speaks about the abomination of desolation and says, in effect, "It is really going to get bad. You don't realize how bad it is really going to get." But Jesus doesn't stop there: "And except those days should be shortened, there should no flesh be saved: but for the elect's sake those days shall be shortened."

Satan's future attempt to completely destroy God's ancient covenant people will fail. Jews living at the time of the abomination of desolation will endure until the Messiah comes for their final deliverance. This is forcefully brought out in Luke 21:24: ". . . and Jerusalem shall be trodden down of the Gentiles, *until the times of the Gentiles be fulfilled.*" Jesus is revealing three things.

First, Jerusalem's fall is of limited duration. It is not final, nor will it be complete.

Second, there *is* a period of time when gentiles will overrun Jerusalem and dominate the city and people.

Third, there will be a time when this situation is radically reversed.

The Lord drives home this point when He says: "And when these things begin to come to pass, then look up, and lift up your heads; *for your redemption draweth nigh.*" Jesus says, "your redemption," not "your destruction." What happened under the Romans in A.D. 70 was destruction, not redemption. Those who want to discredit Bible prophecy, and who sing the song that all prophecy has been fulfilled, have entirely missed the central point of the Olivet Discourse: God will preserve and deliver His people. There is no way that this deliverance happened in A.D. 70.

All of this helps us to understand one of the most highly controverted words of Jesus in the whole New Testament. In Matthew 24:34

we read: "Verily I say unto you, This generation shall not pass, till all these things be fulfilled." Did Jesus mean that everything in the Olivet Discourse would be fulfilled in the lifetime of the apostles? That is precisely the conclusion drawn by some. However, they can only make that conclusion by missing, or deliberately ignoring, the promise of the Olivet Discourse. There was no deliverance for Jerusalem in the first century. There was nothing but destruction. And the same thing happened in the second century with the Bar Kochba revolt. Israel and its religion was humbled. But that's not what Jesus was saying. His point: "The generation that sees the signs signaling My return will endure to see the Messiah." When the signs appear, prophetic events will proceed very quickly.

The Olivet Discourse is speaking about the nearness of the second coming of Christ to the signs that the Lord Jesus has been describing. The generation that sees all these signs will also see the Lord. It is this generation that will not pass away until everything is fulfilled.

Jesus and the Prophecy of the Abomination of Desolation

Jesus makes reference to "the abomination of desolation" in the Olivet Discourse (Matthew 24:15; Mark 13:14). Who or what is this "abomination of desolation"?

In the latter verse in Mark we read: "But when ye shall see the abomination of desolation, spoken of by Daniel the prophet, standing where it ought not, (let him that readeth understand,) then let them that be in Judæa flee to the mountains."

Obviously this "abomination of desolation" is something that signifies great danger, for the scripture follows up the reference to the abomination of desolation with a parenthetical thought in our Lord's discourse inserted by Mark: "(let him that readeth understand,)," which is followed by Jesus' words: "then let them that be in Judæa flee to the mountains."

Who, or what, is Jesus talking about? In his commentary on Mark, William L. Lane explains:

> The Semitic expression used in Daniel describes an abomination so detestable it causes the temple to be abandoned by the people of God and provokes desolation. This mode of expression occurs in passages dealing with persecution and the oppression of the people of God. When the Seleucid ruler Antiochus IV Epiphanes desecrated the temple in 168 B.C. by erecting a small altar dedicated to Zeus over the altar of burnt offering upon which he sacrificed a swine, and made the practice of Judaism a capital offense, it was natural to find a fulfillment of Daniel's prophecy in his action (cf. 1 Maccabees 1:54–59; 6:7). Jesus' use of this distinctive expression, however, indicates that the prophecy was not ultimately fulfilled by the events of the Maccabean period. He warned that there would yet occur an act of profanation so appalling that the temple would be rejected by God as the locus of his glory (cf. Ezekiel 7:14–23). The nature of the profanation is left imprecise, *but the use of the masculine participle to modify a neuter noun suggests that Mark found a personification of the abomination in some concrete figure in history*
> —*The New International Commentary on the New Testament,*
> pp. 466–467; italics supplied by L. Spargimino

Taking these grammatical factors into consideration, the passage could thus be translated: "When you see the abomination that renders the temple unfit for worship *standing in a place where he should not be.* . . ." As Antiochus Epiphanes' pig sacrifice rendered the temple unfit for worship in a past time, so the presence of the Antichrist in the future Tribulation temple will render it unfit for worship. This is corroboration of 2 Thessalonians 2:3–4 which speaks of "that man of sin."

The Tribulation prophesied in the gospels fits in perfectly with the Tribulation as described by the Old Testament prophets. Its focus is Israel's purging and preparation for the millennial kingdom.

The Tribulation Prophesied in Acts

by Noah Hutchings

To continue our appraisal of scriptural evidence that the church will not be in the Tribulation, a period of seven years of war, famine, persecution, and death for millions yet to come, we consider this study of evidence from the Book of Acts.

Luke is referenced as the "beloved physician" (Colossians 4:14), a companion of Paul. Other references indicate that he was from Antioch and may have been a captive servant for a time to a rich Grecian business family. He was also an early disciple of Jesus, and the Book of Acts is a continuance of the Gospel of Luke where we read the connection between the two books ascribed to his authorship in Luke, that the message of the gospel and repentance was to begin in Jerusalem and spread to other nations (Luke 24:46–47): "And said unto them, Thus it is written, and thus it behoved Christ to suffer, and to rise from the dead the third day: And that repentance and remission of sins should be preached in his name among all nations, beginning at Jerusalem." The Book of Acts by Luke relates the rest of the story concerning the spread of the gospel of Jesus Christ to other cities and nations with the coming of the Holy Spirit at Pentecost.

However, a misinterpretation of the Book of Acts by contemporary so-called church scholars presents a gospel story of how the spread of the church age will continue throughout the world until the entire world is Christian and then the church will invite Jesus to come back and rule. Within replacement theology there is no place for a Tribulation period of the nation of Israel in an end-time setting. Nevertheless, the entire scope of Scripture relating to the end of the church age depicts increasing war, famines, earthquakes, apostasy, and the rise of false and apostate religions with the rise of an Antichrist to replace the hope of the second coming. The scriptural prophetic scope depicts this age of increasing judgment on an international scale to end with the Tribulation period, which we know from many prophetic scriptures will last for seven years.

The general scope of the Tribulation as it will relate to Israel and the nations of the world was foretold by Jesus Himself in Matthew 24:15–31.

> When ye therefore shall see the abomination of desolation, spoken of by Daniel the prophet, stand in the holy place, (whoso readeth, let him understand:) Then let them which be in Judæa flee into the mountains: Let him which is on the housetop not come down to take any thing out of his house: Neither let him which is in the field return back to take his clothes. And woe unto them that are with child, and to them that give suck in those days! But pray ye that your flight be not in the winter, neither on the sabbath day: For then shall be great tribulation, such as was not since the beginning of the world to this time, no, nor ever shall be. And except those days should be shortened, there should no flesh be saved: but for the elect's sake those days shall be shortened. Then if any man shall say unto you, Lo, here is Christ, or there; believe it not. For there shall arise false Christs, and false prophets, and shall shew great

signs and wonders; insomuch that, if it were possible, they shall deceive the very elect. Behold, I have told you before. Wherefore if they shall say unto you, Behold, he is in the desert; go not forth: behold, he is in the secret chambers; believe it not. For as the lightning cometh out of the east, and shineth even unto the west; so shall also the coming of the Son of man be. For wheresoever the carcase is, there will the eagles be gathered together. Immediately after the tribulation of those days shall the sun be darkened, and the moon shall not give her light, and the stars shall fall from heaven, and the powers of the heavens shall be shaken: And then shall appear the sign of the Son of man in heaven: and then shall all the tribes of the earth mourn, and they shall see the Son of man coming in the clouds of heaven with power and great glory. And he shall send his angels with a great sound of a trumpet, and they shall gather together his elect from the four winds, from one end of heaven to the other.

We know from the prophecy of the seventy prophetic weeks of Daniel, the ninth chapter, that the Tribulation period will be for seven years. We know from literally hundreds of prophetic scriptures just how the Tribulation period will affect Israel. From my book *Petra in History and Prophecy,* the scriptures are made plain that one-third of Israel will escape when the Antichrist moves against Jerusalem and will be in the city of Petra in Jordan, where I have been many times.

We know from the Book of Revelation and many other related prophecies that there will be a universal law that anyone who resists taking the mark of the Beast and worshipping the Antichrist as god will be beheaded. Israel will escape to Petra, but what about the Christians living in all the nations of the world? It will be a rather simple matter for the Jews to escape to Petra, as this place is just inside Jordan, and for some reason we read that the nation of Jordan will be the one nation of exception that will not be ruled by Antichrist.

Now, the question is presented, Why would God protect the people of Israel from the Antichrist, yet leave His people, the Christians, in the remaining nations of the world to be starved, persecuted, and beheaded? The post-tribulational proponents believe just that. Therefore, Christians must stock up on food and all other necessary life support items for a period of seven years.

We know that there will be a translation of all Christians, at one time and in one body. Whether this applies to a translation of the church, or all Christians alive at the time, or a Rapture, makes little—if any—difference. That at some time in the future every Christian will suddenly be taken up into the air, or sky, to meet Jesus returning with Christians who have died before us, is beyond question, as we read in 1 Thessalonians 4:13–18.

> But I would not have you to be ignorant, brethren, concerning them which are asleep, that ye sorrow not, even as others which have no hope. For if we believe that Jesus died and rose again, even so them also which sleep in Jesus will God bring with him. For this we say unto you by the word of the Lord, that we which are alive and remain unto the coming of the Lord shall not prevent them which are asleep. For the Lord himself shall descend from heaven with a shout, with the voice of the archangel, and with the trump of God: and the dead in Christ shall rise first: Then we which are alive and remain shall be caught up together with them in the clouds, to meet the Lord in the air: and so shall we ever be with the Lord. Wherefore comfort one another with these words.

So the truth of the Rapture is to be a comfort to Christians, not a matter of dispute and contention. However, how much of a comfort could the Rapture be to Christians today if they believe they will go through this seven-year period of tribulation?

Considering the Rapture in relation to the refounding of the kingdom of Israel, we read in Acts 1:7–9:

> And he said unto them, It is not for you to know the times or the seasons, which the Father hath put in his own power. But ye shall receive power, after that the Holy Ghost is come upon you: and ye shall be witnesses unto me both in Jerusalem, and in all Judæa, and in Samaria, and unto the uttermost part of the earth. And when he had spoken these things, while they beheld, he was taken up; and a cloud received him out of their sight.

Israel was refounded as a nation in 1945, but the kingdom identity will not be restored until the temple is again built on its old foundation. The Temple Institute in Jerusalem has rebuilt all the temple vessels, including a giant candlestick, for temple worship just as soon as it is rebuilt. The problem today is that the Muslims are still in control of the Temple Mount where the original Jewish temple stood. In the exact location of the temple is a Muslim shrine, the Dome of the Rock, with a sign on the building, "God had no son." So the Muslims protest that God will send His Son Jesus back to destroy that building and restore the kingdom to Israel.

Both orthodox Jews and fundamental Christians are anxiously waiting for the Jewish temple to be rebuilt, but it cannot be restored as long as the Muslim shrine is on the location. Also, the Scriptures indicate that when it is restored, the Christians will be taken out of the world at the Rapture. This is another reason why we believe the church will not go through the Tribulation.

It is evident from prophetic promises concerning the Rapture of the church there must first be a world government in view, which is already evident today. We read also from the promises of the prophets and the warnings of Jesus in Matthew 24 that there would be wars, earthquakes, pestilences—signs on earth and signs in the heavens concerning the nearness of His coming. Jesus said that already the nearness of His coming could be known, but no one could know the day or the hour. And because the Rapture is associated with the restoration of the temple and kingdom promises to Israel, we read in Acts 1:4–7:

> And, being assembled together with them, commanded them that they should not depart from Jerusalem, but wait for the promise of the Father, which, saith he, ye have heard of me. For John truly baptized with water; but ye shall be baptized with the Holy Ghost not many days hence. When they therefore were come together, they asked of him, saying, Lord, wilt thou at this time restore again the kingdom to Israel? And he said unto them, It is not for you to know the times or the seasons, which the Father hath put in his own power.

We have previously noted that in the third chapter of Acts we find that Jesus Christ must again reign until the restitution of all things. Many Christians believe that once they are saved, their eternal future will be enjoying the beauty and blessings of a heavenly home or a special apartment in the New Jerusalem, but I am not so sure about that. We read in 2 Timothy 2:11–12: "It is a faithful saying: For if we be dead with him, we shall also live with him: If we suffer, we shall also reign with him: if we deny him, he also will deny us."

As we have already noted, in Acts 3 we read that Jesus Christ must reign until the restitution of all things. Therefore, if we are to reign with Jesus Christ in the kingdom we must also serve with Him. And when will the "restitution of all things" be?

We read of all those who are Christians who have received glorified bodies in the Rapture, or resurrection, in Revelation 20:6:

"Blessed and holy is he that hath part in the first resurrection: on such the second death hath no power, but they shall be priests of God and of Christ, and shall reign with him a thousand years."

So the resurrection of Christians at the Rapture should be of great importance to the church. It means that all who are saved will first reign with Jesus Christ in the kingdom age for one thousand years, and then will come the restitution, or glorious perfection, of everything in Heaven and on earth as we read in Revelation 21.

First Thessalonians 5:1–4 reads:

> But of the times and the seasons, brethren, ye have no need that I write unto you. For yourselves know perfectly that the day of the Lord so cometh as a thief in the night. For when they shall say, Peace and safety; then sudden destruction cometh upon them, as travail upon a woman with child; and they shall not escape. But ye, brethren, are not in darkness, that that day should overtake you as a thief.

We read in Revelation 3:10 that the Christians belonging to the church of Philadelphia will be kept from ". . . the hour of temptation, which shall come upon all the world, to try them that dwell upon the earth."

Besides this scripture, there are eight other references from Revelation 4–19 to the Tribulation that will come upon all them "that dwell upon the earth." And who is described as dwelling upon the earth in the Great Tribulation? Israel, nations, the worshippers of Antichrist, martyrs who won't take the mark of the Beast, but no mention of the church as dwellers on the earth.

Nowhere are Christians encouraged to look for Jesus coming with the armies of Heaven or to wait for Him on the Mount of Olives. As indicated in 1 Thessalonians 4:13–18, we will be caught up together, all in one body, to meet Him in the air, and so shall we ever be with the Lord. The calling out of the gentiles as a people for Jesus Christ will be completed at that time, and the dispensation of grace and the church age will end. Forever after that, the church will reign with Jesus Christ as the bride.

Of course, only those who "endure to the end" in the Tribulation will be saved, but Jesus was referring only to those dwelling upon the earth, which does not include the church.

In the epistles, Christians are encouraged only to look for the Lord's coming, be ready for His coming, and be witnessing with a clean testimony when He comes. I get the argument often that we who look for the Rapture are just escapists, sitting around doing nothing, waiting to be taken out of here. At ninety years of age, I still work every day, Monday through Saturday, and fulfill responsibilities in my local church. I have been to eighty-one countries on Bible tours and missions. I am still writing, and still doing one or two programs every day except Sunday. To those who object to the comprehensive word "rapture" because it isn't in the Bible, I would remind them that neither is the word "Bible" in the Bible, or the word "trinity."

To all Christians who have a different understanding about the biblical chronology of our resurrection and translation to heavenly places, I love you anyway and look forward to giving you a holy kiss at the judgment seat of Jesus Christ. Then again, maybe I will just shake your hand.

The Tribulation Prophesied in the Pauline Epistles

by Douglas Stauffer

These times of great skepticism in which we live have infiltrated the church and begun to permeate many of its teachings. Every major doctrine is under attack today, including the next great event in God's prophetic timetable—the Rapture of the church. People today are more frequently questioning whether or not the church will go through the Tribulation. It is important to note that the Apostle Paul's instructions to the church never once mention preparing for the Tribulation. Yet, these are the primary books given to govern the lives of those who make up the church. Does it not seem likely that God would have led Paul to write to the church on how to prepare for, or get through, the Tribulation if this is the true destiny of Christians?

To avoid misunderstanding future events, Bible students must incorporate a three-pronged approach to interpreting prophecy. They must: (1) distinguish between Israel and the church; (2) understand the timing of the events of the books of Revelation and Daniel; and (3) grasp the promised restoration of the nation of Israel.

Some critics of the pre-tribulation Rapture attribute its origin to the teachings of John Nelson Darby and the C. I. Scofield Reference System of the Bible. These assertions are unfounded, though any particular doctrine's longevity does not, by itself, attest to its truthfulness. God reveals His truths to the world using His own timetable and agents. The Book of Ephesians points out that the manifold wisdom of God is made *known by the church:* "To the intent that now unto the principalities and powers in heavenly places might be *known by the church the manifold wisdom of God"* (Ephesians 3:10).

For this reason, history reveals a progressive revelation through time born out of the Word of God. Some believers teach that if the first century church fathers did not teach, preach, or write concerning any particular matter, it cannot be so. They surmise that anything new must be false. Nothing could be further from the truth. God has always progressively revealed His truths when man needed them. Could anyone in the first, or even the nineteenth, century have taught that the mark of the Beast could likely be a computer chip placed *IN* the right hand or *IN* one's forehead? "And he causeth all, both small and great, rich and poor, free and bond, to receive a mark in their right hand, or in their foreheads" (Revelation 13:16).

No writer for the last fifty-nine hundred years ever wrote specifically about Social Security numbers, computer chips, RFID (**R**adio **F**requency **ID**entification) chips, VeriChips, cashless societies, brain scans, or biometrics, so how could this be a fulfillment of end-times prophecy, since these concepts do not precede the current or last century? Christians prior to the current generation had no concept of satellites or surveillance cameras and drones used to spy and kill remotely. All of these gadgets have emerged to help prepare the world for the end times. However, it is just as likely that the world could experience a high-altitude nuclear electromagnetic pulse (HEMP), wiping out all electronic equipment, and necessitating the return of swords, horses, and guillotines as predicted.

Pre-/Mid-/Post-Tribulation

There are four major viewpoints concerning the timing of the Rapture in relation to the Tribulation. The *pre-tribulational* view reveals that the church is gathered together out of the world prior to the onset of the Tribulation. This teaching also emphasizes that God's focus will shift away from the church (no longer on earth) to Israel and its national restoration.

Those not giving the Bible the preeminence demanded by God hatched the next three viewpoints. The *mid-tribulational* and *pre-wrath* views speculate that the Rapture occurs three and a half years into the Tribulation. The *post-tribulational* view claims that the church is raptured following the Tribulation. These erroneous views cause many problems. If the Rapture takes place at the end of the Tribulation, and Christ destroys all *unbelievers* at His second coming before the millennium, there is no one left with natural bodies to populate the earth during the one thousand-year reign of Christ.

According to Bible *eschatology* (doctrines concerning future events), there are four groups of people occupying the millennium:

1. Present-day believers with glorified bodies ruling as joint-heirs with Christ over those with natural bodies (Revelation 20:6).
2. Tribulation believers killed during the Tribulation but resurrected before the millennium, who now have glorified bodies (Revelation 7:13–14; 20:4).
3. Tribulation survivors who were a blessing to Israel (Matthew 25:32–40). This group will bear children with natural bodies during the millennium which are still subject to sin and death.
4. Many of these people at the end of the thousand years will rebel against King Jesus (Isaiah 65:20; Revelation 20:7–9).

Who populates the millennium? If the Rapture takes place at the *END* of the Tribulation, there will be no believers remaining on earth with natural bodies. The Bible teaches that *many* nations will populate the millennium (Zechariah 14:16–19; Revelation 20:8). Where do they come from, if not from the Tribulation? Those who populate the millennium consist of individuals who survive the Tribulation period without being killed or taking the mark of the Beast.

Pictures and Types

Simply because a teaching is new does not make it fraudulent. God is supreme and chooses to express His truths using whatever method He desires. Enoch and Noah provide an excellent example of the contrast between the Rapture and the second coming.

Enoch and Noah. Enoch is a type of the church. He saw the horrors of the flood on the horizon, yet he was caught up to Heaven *without dying* (Genesis 5:24). Noah, on the other hand, is a picture of the Tribulation saint. He went through God's worldwide judgment with God's supernatural protection. Noah's reward: he is still on earth on the other side of the flood. His survival pictures the earthly people who make it through the Tribulation and enter into the millennium.

On the other hand, after the judgment, Enoch is still in Paradise. He pictures the church, the heavenly people (Ephesians 1:3; 2:6; Philippians 3:20). It is important to note that the church never usurped promises to Israel but is given its own set of promises as a heavenly people. One of these promises is to miss the wrath of God poured out upon the world during the Tribulation.

Joshua. Joshua provides a case in point, where a truth cannot be seen until God provides man with an English Bible divided into chapters. The first English Bible was Wycliffe in 1384. It is important to note that the Old Testament was not divided into chapters until 1445, and the New Testament in 1555.

Sometimes God uses Bible numerics to verify the most debated topics. Here is an example of using the number of man (#6) and the Old Testament to validate the pre-tribulational Rapture of the church. The sixth (#6) book of the Bible is Joshua. Joshua contains six (#6) letters, and it is the first book named after a man. Due to the chapter and verse divisions, this is the first time numerically that the mark of the Beast shows up in Scripture. Here is the sixth book **(6)**, sixth chapter **(6)**, sixth verse **(6)**, or **(666)**: "And Joshua the son of Nun called the priests, and said unto them, Take up the ark of the covenant, and let seven priests bear *seven trumpets* of rams' horns before the ark of the LORD" (Joshua 6:6)

If Joshua 6:6 numerically represents the mark of the Beast (the sixth book [6], sixth chapter [6] and sixth verse [6] = 666), a pre-tribulationist (or futurist) would expect to find a depiction of the Rapture of the church (in type) *PRIOR* to the occurrence of this **666**. The Bible does, in fact, depict the Rapture which is described in 1 Thessalonians 4 in the verse preceding the **666**. "And it shall come to pass, that when they make a long blast with the ram's horn, and when ye hear the sound of the *trumpet,* all the people shall *shout* with a great shout; and the wall of the city shall fall down flat, and *the people shall ascend up* every man straight before him" (Joshua 6:5).

Compare the "trumpet" in Joshua 6 to the "trump" in 1 Thessalonians; the "shout" to the "shout"; and the "people shall ascend up" to Christians "caught up . . . to meet the Lord in the air": "For the Lord himself shall descend from heaven with a *shout,* with the voice of the archangel, and with the *trump* of God: and the dead in Christ shall rise first: Then we which are alive and remain shall be *caught up* together with them in the clouds, *to meet the Lord in the air:* and so shall we ever be with the Lord" (1 Thessalonians 4:16–17).

Is all of this mere coincidence, or is God also sovereign when it comes to the English Bible and His desire to use any and all means to display His glory? You should also take note of the "seven trumpets" mentioned in Joshua 6:6 which correspond to the Tribulation's seven trumpets that begin sounding after the opening of the seventh seal in Revelation 8. "And the seven angels which had the *seven trumpets* prepared themselves to sound" (Revelation 8:6).

The Apostle John. The Apostle John represents one of the many types of the church found in the Word of God. Five times John was singled out among the apostles as the disciple whom Jesus "loved" (John 13:23; 19:26; 20:2; 21:7, 20). In a parallel fashion to the love Christ displayed toward John, the Apostle Paul develops five aspects of Christ's love for the church in Ephesians 5:25–29. Paul points out Christ's PASSIONATE love for the church (vs. 25); His PURIFYING love for the church (vs. 26); His PRESENTING love for the church (vs. 27); His PROTECTING love for the church (vs. 28); and His PROVIDING love for the church (vs. 29). Is there any wonder why God refers to the church as His "beloved"? "Put on therefore, as the elect of God, *holy and beloved*, bowels of mercies, kindness, humbleness of mind, meekness, longsuffering" (Colossians 3:12).

The Lord refers to His special love for both John and the church. John's ascent into Heaven in Revelation 4:1–2 offers another type of the pre-tribulation Rapture of the church. God conspicuously located John's ascent into Heaven to further confirm the timing of the Rapture. As recorded in Revelation, John heard the voice of God speaking like a "trumpet" calling him up to Heaven. This represents an event that takes place chronologically between the church *on earth* (Revelation 1:4, 11, 20; 2:1, 7–8, 11–12, 17–18, 23, 29; 3:1, 6–7, 13–14, 22) and the church *in Heaven* (Revelation 4–5).

The Lord transported John, Christ's beloved apostle (Revelation 1:10), to a time almost two centuries into the future. Following true historical chronology, John is transported (raptured) into Heaven in Revelation 4:1–2. This takes place after writing to the seven churches in Asia Minor (Revelation 2–3), with this writing representative of the seven periods of church history.

John's experience parallels what believers will encounter upon Christ's return for the church. "Trump" is found only twice in the Bible, both times in Paul's writings to the church. This clearly distinguishes it from the seven "trumpets" found in Revelation 8. The Bible says that we shall not all sleep (die), but shall all be changed "at the last trump." "In a moment, in the twinkling of an eye, *at the last trump:* for the trumpet shall sound, and the dead shall be raised incorruptible, and we shall be changed" (1 Corinthians 15:52).

This reference to "the last *trump"* cannot be the last of the seven *trumpets* blown by an angel signaling the end of the Tribulation (Revelation 11:15) unless the church goes through the entire Tribulation and suffers the wrath of Almighty God. This trump refers to the final sound at the end of the church age called the *"trump* of God" (1 Thessalonians 4:16). This coincides to the Spirit's transporting of John. "I was in the Spirit on the Lord's day, and *heard behind me a great voice, as of a trumpet"* (Revelation 1:10).

This chronology concerning John is further proof that the "trump" referred to by Paul cannot be synonymous with the last trumpet of the Tribulation. If it were the same, then church age believers would be on earth for all seven seals, seven trumpets, and seven vials, etc. In other words, the church would endure all of God's *wrath* poured out upon the inhabitants of earth.

John's Writings: Past, Present, and Future

The Lord instructs the Apostle John to cover three time periods in his writings in Revelation: past, present, and future. "Write the things which thou *hast seen,* and the things which *are,* and the things which *shall be* hereafter" (Revelation 1:19).

First, John writes concerning the things *"which thou hast seen"* (the past) covered by the eyewitness revelation of events. This would include the historical events during the church age through the Rapture (represented by the prophetic application to church history of the literal churches in Revelation 2–4).

The *"things which are,"* for John, would be the time period immediately following the Rapture of the church, when he finds himself in Heaven, in Revelation 4. He has already heard the "trump of God" that took place in Revelation 1:10, a trump that is "behind" him, according to the chronological flow of the scriptures.

Thus, the *"things which are"* would include the church age believers in Heaven (Revelation 4–5) and the Tribulation period simultaneously taking place on earth, witnessed firsthand and recorded in Revelation 6–19.

It is also very important to note that the church does not show up anywhere in these fourteen chapters comprising the account of the Tribulation period on earth. The church reappears with Christ, following Him from Heaven *after* the Tribulation. "And the armies which were in heaven followed him upon white horses, clothed in fine linen, white and clean" (Revelation 19:14).

The third time period covers the *"things which shall be hereafter."* John's writings concerning the future cover the millennium and eternity (Revelation 20–22).

Imminent Return

Christ's return could happen at any time. This is not known as much by what we read in the newspapers (though quite revealing), but rather by what the Bible teaches us. God wrote the Bible so that every generation of Christians would believe that the Lord Jesus Christ could come in their day, at any moment, at any time, without the necessity of any prophecies being fulfilled prior to His return.

Christians are to live with an expectancy that today could be the day. We are told to *wait for* and *look for* Christ's return. If certain events must occur prior to His return for the church, then His "imminent return" is anything but imminent. If the church is to go through any part of Daniel's seventieth week, instead of looking for "that blessed hope" (Titus 2:13), we had better be preparing for survival. However, pre-tribulationism clearly distinguishes between the church today and Israel in the future, as well as their respective earthly interactions with God. Should Christians be as focused on moral and political reform as they are on the souls of the lost? Will part of the church be forced to endure the judgment cast down upon Israel's sins (during the Tribulation) while the vast majority of the church has already gone on to be with the Lord?

Ambassadors Called Home

The Bible proclaims a future two-stage coming of Christ. This involves: (1) His return to rapture the church *prior* to the Tribulation; and (2) His return to set up His literal, physical kingdom on earth *following* the Tribulation. Unfortunately, Bible prophecy teachers all too often confuse the end-times signs occurring prior to the Rapture. Many of the signs involving spiritual degeneration (2 Timothy 3) and physical degeneration (Matthew 24) precede the Rapture. Misunderstanding these signs has caused some Bible teachers to conclude that the church must expect to go through the Tribulation. Such indicators as the one-world monetary and governmental systems add to their confusion.

The Tribulation, along with the second coming, involves a future timetable with a definite starting point, a definite duration, and a definite ending point. The Tribulation includes the abomination of desolation (Matthew 24:15–16), lasts seven years, and ends at the return of Christ to the Mount of Olives (Zechariah 14:4). This return to the Mount of Olives is the second coming when the mountain shall cleave in two.

On the other hand, the Bible defines the timing of the Rapture as imminent and describes the child of God as anticipating it, yet having no idea as to its timing. One thing is for sure: before God declares war on this world, He is going to call home His ambassadors. His embassies will be closed once and for all. "Now then we are *ambassadors for Christ,* as though God did beseech you by us: we pray you in Christ's stead, be ye reconciled to God" (2 Corinthians 5:20).

As an ambassador for Christ during the church age, the individual believer preaches the *ministry of reconciliation,* telling lost people to be reconciled to God by trusting in the finished work of Jesus Christ on the cross of Calvary.

The Tribulation deals with Israel's transgression against God (Daniel 9:5, 11, 14, etc.) and their collective *reconciliation* as a nation. The summation of the matter is given toward the end of Daniel 9. "Seventy weeks are determined upon thy people [Israel] and upon thy holy city [Jerusalem], *to finish the transgression,* and to make an *end of sins,* and to *make reconciliation for iniquity,* and to bring in everlasting righteousness, and to seal up the vision and prophecy, and to anoint the most Holy" (Daniel 9:24).

Look and Wait!

The primary church age epistles refer to Jesus' imminent return by making statements about the believer's reaction to it. Paul tells the church to be "looking for" and "waiting for" the appearing and coming of Christ (that blessed hope). *"Looking for* that blessed hope, and the glorious *appearing* of the great God and our Saviour Jesus Christ" (Titus 2:13). "So that ye come behind in no gift; *waiting for* the *coming* of our Lord Jesus Christ" (1 Corinthians 1:7).

Why would the church's attention be directed toward His return if so much must take place prior to His showing up? Additionally, Paul tells the church to "look for" and be patiently "waiting for" Christ to return. "For our conversation is in heaven; from whence also we *look for* the Saviour, the Lord Jesus Christ" (Philippians 3:20). "And the Lord direct your hearts into the love of God, and into the patient *waiting for* Christ" (2 Thessalonians 3:5).

Paul instructs the Christian to "watch," so that "that day" does not overtake us as a thief. "But ye, brethren, are not in darkness, *that that day* should overtake you as a thief. Ye are all the children of light, and the children of the day: we are not of the night, nor of darkness. Therefore let us not sleep, as do others; but let us *watch* and be sober" (1 Thessalonians 5:4–6).

Paul distinguishes between "ye," "you," and "us" versus "they" and "them" in the opening three verses of this chapter. The church looking for and waiting for Christ hardly sounds like we are first going through the Tribulation. If the church was destined to go through the Tribulation, we should actually be looking for the abomination of desolation (Matthew 24:15), the two witnesses (Revelation 11:3), and the 144,000 (Revelation 7:4; 14:3) to show up. Paul emphasizes again and again that we are looking for Christ's APPEARING and our subsequent DISAPPEARING.

Kings and Priests

The Apostle Paul mentions the Christian in relation to Christ's *appearing* seven times. In the book of 2 Timothy he emphasizes the difference between the two resurrections, referring to the first resurrection at His *appearing* and the second at His *kingdom*. "I charge thee therefore before God, and the Lord Jesus Christ, who shall judge the quick and the dead at his *appearing and his kingdom"* (2 Timothy 4:1).

The *appearing* of Christ in the clouds to catch away the church certainly does not match up to His second coming, when He will set up His kingdom on earth. Six more times the Apostle Paul mentions Christ's appearing:

» "When *Christ,* who is our life, *shall appear,* then shall ye also appear with him in glory" (Colossians 3:4).
» "That thou keep this commandment without spot, unrebukeable, until the *appearing of our Lord Jesus Christ"* (1 Timothy 6:14).
» "But is now made manifest by the *appearing of our Saviour Jesus Christ,* who hath abolished death, and hath brought life and immortality to light through the gospel" (2 Timothy 1:10).
» "Looking for that blessed hope, and the glorious *appearing of the great God and our Saviour Jesus Christ"* (Titus 2:13).
» "Henceforth there is laid up for me a *crown of righteousness,* which the Lord, the righteous judge, shall give me at that day: and not to me only, but unto all them also that love *his appearing"* (2 Timothy 4:8).

Take note of the "crown of righteousness." Crowns are promised to the church and issued at the judgment seat of Christ. Notice the apparel of the elders before the throne after the Rapture depicted in Revelation 4. "And round about the throne were four and twenty seats: and upon the seats I saw four and twenty elders sitting, *clothed in white raiment;* and they had on their heads *crowns of gold"* (Revelation 4:4).

These elders are clothed in *white raiment* (the attire of a priest) with *crowns* (worn by kings) on their heads. Will those rewarded at the judgment seat of Christ be clothed in white raiment casting their crowns too? Paul points out that God promises Christians to be joint-heirs with Him and reign with Him on earth. Revelation points out that believers will be kings (crowns) and priests (white raiment) (Revelation 1:6). Here is the scene in Heaven after the Rapture of Revelation 4. "And hast made us unto our God *kings and priests:* and we shall *reign on the earth*" (Revelation 5:10).

No Levitical Old Testament priest ever wore a crown or sat upon a throne; however, this is the perfect description of a *royal priesthood* (1 Peter 2:9). The royal priesthood identifies a king and priest, which is not Israel but the church!

Rapture Defined

The moment the Rapture takes place, those who are *in Christ* (dead and alive) will have their "vile" bodies changed into new, glorified immortal bodies (Philippians 3:21). The Rapture is similar to events that happened to other Bible characters, such as Enoch (Genesis 5:24; Hebrews 11:5), Elijah (2 Kings 2:11), Jesus (Acts 1:9), and the future two witnesses (Revelation 11:12).

The Lord's Return

One of the distinguishing differences between the Rapture (preceding the Tribulation) and the second coming (following the Tribulation) concerns the Lord's return. At the Rapture, Christians meet the Lord *in the air;* therefore, when Christ returns at the Rapture He does not set foot on the Mount of Olives, as foretold concerning His second coming to earth. The church meets Him in the air. "Then we which are alive and remain shall be caught up together with them in the clouds, *to meet the Lord in the air:* and so shall we ever be with the Lord" (1 Thessalonians 4:17).

The church "meet[ing] the Lord in the air" stands in stark contrast to Christ's standing upon the earth at His second coming. At the second coming, no one meets Him in the air. "And *his feet shall stand in that day upon the mount of Olives,* which is before Jerusalem on the east, and the mount of Olives shall cleave in the midst thereof toward the east and toward the west, and there shall be a very great valley; and half of the mountain shall remove toward the north, and half of it toward the south" (Zechariah 14:4).

Exclusivity

The majority of Bible history primarily revolves around the nation of Israel, beginning with Abraham and continuing through the early part of the Book of Acts. Future prophecy also deals primarily with the Jewish nation. Parenthetically, God is dealing with the church. The church includes both Jew and gentile, though any distinction is eliminated within this body of believers. *"There is neither Jew nor Greek,* there is neither bond nor free, there is neither male nor female: *for ye are all one in Christ Jesus"* (Galatians 3:28).

The church age encompasses God's interaction with His church and ends as the church is caught up to Heaven in the Rapture. The Rapture is exclusive, as it only involves those who are *in Christ,* whether they have already died or yet remain alive until His return. Here is a sampling of the many verses demonstrating that those *in Christ* are the church:

» "Therefore if any man be *in Christ...*" (2 Corinthians 5:17).

- » "So we, being many, are one body *in Christ* . . ." (Romans 12:5).
- » ". . . *in Christ* shall all be made alive" (1 Corinthians 15:22).
- » "For *in Christ Jesus* . . ." (Galatians 6:15).
- » "Salute every saint *in Christ Jesus* . . ." (Philippians 4:21).

The Rapture does *not* involve the nation of Israel as a whole and excludes the earth's inhabitants who have rejected Christ as Saviour. All pre-tribulationists know and teach that it is the unbelievers who are left behind at the Rapture of the church from this earth. The Book of Jeremiah refers to the Tribulation as the time of "Jacob's trouble." Jacob is Israel! Israel is not the church. "Alas! for *that day is great, so that none is like it: it is even the time of Jacob's trouble;* but he [Jacob, renamed Israel] shall be *saved out of it*" (Jeremiah 30:7).

Reading the context of this passage reveals that God will again focus on His people. Israel is saved OUT OF IT (the Tribulation) and the church is saved FROM IT (the Tribulation). Those "in Christ" need not be concerned about the time of Jacob's trouble. The Tribulation is a time of judgment, preparation, and restoration for Israel. The purpose *is not* to prepare the church for glory or to punish the church for growing cold. The church never replaced Israel, nor do they usurp God's promises or prophecies concerning them. The prayer Jesus told His listeners to pray is a case in point. "But pray ye that your flight be not in the winter, neither on the *sabbath day:* For then shall be great tribulation, such as was not since the beginning of the world to this time, no, nor ever shall be" (Matthew 24:20).

Why would anyone in the church pray that his flight would not be on the Sabbath day? The Apostle Paul writes concerning the church age believers' relationship to the Sabbath. *"Let no man therefore judge you* in meat, or in drink, or in respect of an holyday, or of the new moon, or *of the sabbath days:* Which are a shadow of things to come; but the body is of Christ" (Colossians 2:16–17).

The church certainly does not need to be concerned that our flight not be on the Sabbath since the Sabbath deals only with Israel and never the church.

After the Rapture, God is going to break the yoke from off the necks of His chosen people, and once again restore them to their rightful place. The two witnesses, representing the *prophets* (Elijah) and the *Law* (Moses) will return, and God will choose 144,000 male Jewish virgins to preach the gospel of the kingdom throughout the world and then the end comes. "And *this gospel of the kingdom shall be preached* in all the world for a witness unto all nations; and *then shall the end come*" (Matthew 24:14).

"This gospel of the kingdom" is not synonymous with "the gospel of the grace of God" (Acts 20:24) preached by Paul, along with every believer for almost two thousand years. If the church remains during the Tribulation and things do not revert back to Israel, then these Jews preaching the gospel of the kingdom are accursed according to the scripture. "As we said before, so say I now again, *If any man preach any other gospel unto you than that ye have received, let him be accursed*" (Galatians 1:9).

Tribulation Defined

The Bible describes the horrifying conditions that will exist during the Tribulation following the Rapture. The Tribulation consists of *one week* (of years) or a seven-year period (Daniel 9:27) that evolves into utter chaos on the earth. The Antichrist will rise to power and institute a new world order and one-world government during the time of Jacob's trouble. Those who refuse to take the mark of the Beast will be *beheaded* (Revelation 20:4).

With the Antichrist in full control, God will pour out His wrath upon the earth through the seven seal judgments. The Tribulation will end with the gathering of the nations to the Battle of Armageddon (Revelation 16:16), where Christ will return victoriously, commencing His one thousand-year millennial reign on the throne of David in Jerusalem (Revelation 20:2–7).

The removal of the church precedes divine judgment inflicted upon the world. God's Word offers many such historical patterns. Examples include Enoch's escape prior to the flood, Lot's removal from Sodom prior to the fire and brimstone, and Rahab's protection prior to the destruction of Jericho. Peter reveals the mind of the Lord on the matter, as he points out Lot's deliverance (2 Peter 2:7) and God's proclamation: "The Lord knoweth how to deliver the godly out of temptations, and to reserve the unjust unto the day of judgment to be punished" (verse 9).

Some mid-tribulationists develop unscriptural arguments attempting to avoid a problem of their own making. Some of them teach that the Tribulation is the wrath of Satan on man (misapplying Revelation 12:12), but the Bible clearly defines the Tribulation as "the great day of [God's] wrath." "For *the great day of his wrath* is come; and who shall be able to stand?" (Revelation 6:17).

Fourteen times the Bible emphasizes that the Tribulation involves an outpouring of God's *wrath*. A sampling of scriptural proof:

» wrath of God (Revelation 14:10, 19);
» his wrath (Revelation 16:19; and
» wrath of Almighty God (Revelation 19:15).

Similar to Lot and his *family,* and Rahab and her *family,* God's *family* (Ephesians 3:15) will be removed prior to the outpouring of God's wrath. The church will be delivered from wrath because it is not appointed to wrath: "And to wait for his Son from heaven, whom he raised from the dead, even Jesus, which *delivered us from the wrath to come"* (1 Thessalonians 1:10). "For *God hath not appointed us to wrath*, but to obtain salvation by our Lord Jesus Christ" (1 Thessalonians 5:9).

What's coming to the earth? The wrath of Almighty God! Since Jesus delivered us from the "wrath to come," why would He leave us here to experience the day of God's wrath? *"The great day of the* LORD *is near, it is near, and hasteth greatly, even the voice of the day of the* LORD*: the mighty man shall cry there bitterly. That day is a day of wrath, a day of trouble and distress, a day of wasteness and desolation, a day of darkness and gloominess, a day of clouds and thick darkness"* (Zephaniah 1:14–15).

Lot is the definitive example. Nobody in Sodom considered Lot to be righteous, but God testifies that it was so. Even Lot's family members mocked him when he warned them of God's impending wrath. It is important to note that God would not send judgment to Sodom and Gomorrah until he got every righteous person out of that city—righteous in God's eyes. "And delivered *just Lot*, vexed with the filthy conversation of the wicked: (For *that righteous man* dwelling among them, in seeing and hearing, vexed his righteous soul from day to day with their unlawful deeds)" (2 Peter 2:7–8).

Lot got out before God's judgment fell, though he was only removed because he was justified (just). God could not send the judgment until he got Lot out of harm's way. The message of the Lord's return for the church is a message of hope, encouragement, and comfort, not one of fear and wrath. The church will not be removed because the world views us as righteous, but because God does.

The Day of Christ

Far too many Bible teachers have simply parroted what they have been taught concerning the theme of 2 Thessalonians 2. These teachings have further resulted in a wide array of incorrect traditions. Some men have even changed the scripture, thinking to correct "God's error" in the text.

The passage begins by positively focusing on the "brethren" and the "Lord Jesus Christ." It then shifts 180 degrees to the "mystery of iniquity" encompassing the man of sin, the son of perdition, the Wicked and Satan, himself. The "mystery of iniquity" is the antithesis to the "mystery of godliness" (1 Timothy 3:16).

Paul begins the chapter by addressing a counterfeit letter supposedly from him that had confused the Thessalonica believers. The imposter had written to them claiming they had missed the Rapture (or the "gathering together"). Understanding the first two verses helps to establish the foundation that the next ten verses build upon. "Now we beseech you, brethren, by the *coming* of our Lord Jesus Christ, and by our *gathering together* unto him, That ye be not soon shaken in mind, or be troubled, neither by spirit, nor by word, nor by *letter* as from us, as that the *day of Christ* is *at hand"* (2 Thessalonians 2:1–2).

In Paul's previous epistle to the Thessalonians, he had clearly expounded to them the Lord's "coming" and the believer's gathering "together with him" (1 Thessalonians 4:13–18). In this letter he told them that they would be in His "presence . . . at his coming" (1 Thessalonians 2:19). For this reason, all believers are commanded to be "waiting" for His imminent return (1 Corinthians 1:7). Truly, these Thessalonians had been suffering a "great trial of affliction" similar to those saints in Corinth (2 Corinthians 8:2).

But what were they to make of this confusing and contradictory letter supposedly from Paul? Had these believers really missed the "gathering together" of the church? It is important to note that the day of Christ (2 Thessalonians 1:10) refers to events *in Heaven* following the Rapture (1 Corinthians 3:13; Philippians 1:6, 10; 2:16) but may also include simultaneous events *on earth* through the second coming of Christ (2 Thessalonians 1:7–9). Another example is 2 Timothy 1:12, 18.

These are some of the issues addressed in Paul's second letter to the Thessalonians. If Paul had been referring to the Rapture as NOT "at hand," he would have been contradicting what he had already written to the Romans concerning that day being at hand. "The night is far spent, *the day is at hand:* let us therefore cast off the works of darkness, and let us put on the armour of light" (Romans 13:12).

In this second letter to the Thessalonians, Paul sets out to assure these faithful followers of the Lord that they had *not* missed the Rapture. Continuing: "Let no man deceive you by any means [including a letter supposedly from the Apostle Paul]: for that day [the day of Christ in verse 2] shall not come, except there come a *falling away* first, and that *man of sin be revealed,* the *son of perdition;* Who opposeth and exalteth himself above all that is called God, or that is worshipped; so that he as God sitteth in the temple of God, shewing himself that he is God" (2 Thessalonians 2:3–4).

The "falling away" here is not simply a reference to the last-days prophecy of perilous times (2 Timothy 3:1). Instead, it likely references one of two bands of people: (1) those who in time of temptation "fall away" (Luke 8:13), lacking the appropriate foundation, or (2) those taken into captivity (Jeremiah 37:13–14; 39:9; 52:15). The Book of Hebrews also mentions those who *"fall away"* in Hebrews 6:6, pointing out that it is impossible to renew them again.

The falling away precedes the revelation of the man of sin. The *man of sin* is *the son of perdition* who opposes all that is worshipped and exalts himself above God. As the ultimate imposter, he will sit as god in the temple of God, showing himself that he is god. Jesus identified the "son of perdition" in His day (John 17:12) as one who Satan incarnated (Luke 22:3). Peter said Judas went to his own place (Acts 1:25). John identifies the place (Revelation 9:11) and prophesies the return of a Satan-indwelled man (Revelation 17:8). Satan's ultimate demise will take place when he once again takes upon himself a body of flesh.

Paul cautioned the Thessalonians not to be shaken, troubled, or deceived. He now continues by admonishing them not to be forgetful. Continuing: "Remember ye not, that, when I was yet with you, I told you these things? And *now ye know what withholdeth* that he might be revealed in his time" (2 Thessalonians 2:5–6).

In verse 6, Paul tells the Thessalonians that they NOW know WHAT "withholdeth" (or is holding back) the revealing of the man of sin. It is the "Spirit of Christ" (Romans 8:9) indwelling the believers who make up the church. Studying how God has historically worked offers the biblical precedent and pattern.

What withholdeth? The Thessalonians know "what withholdeth." "Withheld" is first used in Genesis 20:6 referring to God withholding a lost man (Abimelech) from sin. By applying the Bible *rule of first mention*, we see that the Spirit of Christ which indwells every believer now restrains the world from the grievous sin prophesied to follow the Rapture of the church.

During the church age, the Spirit of Christ indwells the believer, directing his life unless grieved or quenched by the Christian. By removing the church, the Spirit of God remains in the world because He is omnipresent (Psalm 139:7–10); however, His role shifts dramatically. Revelation points out that the Spirit of God will still be working during the Tribulation, for instance, here, with the resurrection of the two witnesses. "And after three days and an half *the Spirit of life from God entered into them*, and they stood upon their feet; and great fear fell upon them which saw them" (Revelation 11:11).

Combining this first usage of "withholdeth" in Genesis with another picture offers further proof for applying *the withholding* to the church (believers indwelt by the Spirit of Christ). This second example of "withholden" involves David's preparing to pour out his wrath upon "innocent blood" (1 Samuel 25:26). David is *withholden* by Abigail (a picture of the church) while she remains yoked to Nabal (a picture of the world). She restrains David (a type of Christ's return) for a set period of time. After this time is complete, David marries Abigail once she is removed from Nabal and brought to David. These prophetic pictures and types shine light upon the mysteries unrecognizable to those lacking faith in the Scriptures. Continuing: "For the *mystery of iniquity* doth already work: only he who now letteth will let, until he be taken out of the way. And then shall *that Wicked* be revealed, whom the Lord shall consume with the spirit of his mouth, and shall destroy with the brightness of his coming: Even him, whose coming is after the working of Satan with all power and signs and lying wonders" (2 Thessalonians 2:7–9).

The "mystery of iniquity" does not refer to a particular person like the "man of sin," but more of an association involving the wickedness controlled by Satan throughout the centuries. It is said to be a mystery because a mystery remains a mystery until revealed. This mystery of iniquity was simply a previously UNREVEALED truth. When the church is taken out of the way, then the mystery of iniquity is revealed, which is "that Wicked." "That Wicked" is defined elsewhere as the "wicked one": "The field is the world; the good seed are the children of the kingdom; but the *tares* are the *children of the wicked one*" (Matthew 13:38). "Not as *Cain,* who was *of that wicked one,* and slew his brother. And wherefore slew he him? Because his own works were evil, and his brother's righteous" (1 John 3:12).

The "mystery of iniquity" is presently working through the "man of sin." After the Rapture of the church, that wicked one, Satan's seed (Genesis 3:15) shall be revealed in all his glory.

The Reign with Christ

As we have seen, the Apostle John travels into the future (Revelation

1:19) finding himself time-warped past the church age, with the Rapture just behind him (Revelation 4:1–2), and at the onset of the Tribulation and the second coming. The millennium and eternity are yet in the *future*. Thereafter, the church is no longer mentioned as being ON EARTH, but IN HEAVEN. "And they [the saints of verse 8] sung a new song, saying, Thou art worthy to take the book, and to open the seals thereof: for thou wast slain, and hast *redeemed us* to God by thy blood out of every kindred, and tongue, and people, and nation; And hast made us unto our God kings and priests: and *we shall reign on the earth*" (Revelation 5:9–10).

If this is not the church, then who are these saints in Heaven before the Tribulation who will reign ON THE EARTH in the future? Christians are promised to be *joint-heirs* with Christ, so long as we know Him, the power of His resurrection through salvation. In order to *reign* with Him, we must be partakers in the "fellowship of his sufferings" (Philippians 3:10). It is the church that will one day reign with Christ as joint-heirs, individually rewarded for living for Him (and suffering for Him) on this earth. Here are a few of the church age promises associated with suffering and reigning:

» "And if children, then heirs; heirs of God, and *joint-heirs with Christ;* if so be that we *suffer* with him, that we may be also glorified together. For I reckon that the sufferings of this present time are not worthy to be compared with the glory which shall be revealed in us" (Romans 8:17–18).
» "If we suffer, *we shall also reign with him:* if we deny him, he also will deny us" (2 Timothy 2:12).
» "Yea, and all that will live *godly* in Christ Jesus shall *suffer persecution*" (2 Timothy 3:12).

We are to be "partakers of the sufferings" (2 Corinthians 1:5–7), lest we "suffer loss" at the judgment seat of Christ (1 Corinthians 3:15). We are promised a reign with Him, but not for those who refuse to live for Him on earth. Christians who live for God will suffer tribulation (2 Peter 2:19–20; 3:17). Those who live for self will not only suffer in this life, but will also suffer the loss of rewards in the next.

Suffering Tribulation

Suffering and tribulation go hand in hand. The word tribulation(s) is found in the Bible twenty-six times in twenty-five verses, with twenty-one occurrences in the New Testament. It is important to distinguish between the period of time referred to as the Tribulation or the Great Tribulation, and a Christian who suffers or goes through some type of tribulation.

The Bible refers to tribulation several times, but the *Great Tribulation* only twice (Matthew 24:21; Revelation 7:14). The Bible refers to the Tribulation simply as "the *tribulation*" two additional times (Matthew 24:29; Mark 13:24).

The Apostle Paul refers to *tribulation* as a way of life for Christians living godly in this world (Romans 5:3; 8:35; 12:12; 2 Corinthians 1:4; 7:4; Ephesians 3:13; 1 Thessalonians 3:4; 2 Thessalonians 1:4), and an inevitable consequence for the lost man reaping what he has sown (Romans 2:9; 2 Thessalonians 1:6). However, the Apostle Paul never once refers to the Great Tribulation or Tribulation as a future period of time for the church.

Believers are going to experience "tribulation," but only those conspiring to set forth a false doctrinal agenda would apply these references of suffering tribulation to that set period of time known as the Great Tribulation. Christians will suffer, and they will suffer persecution and tribulation.

Yet, it is dishonest and dangerous exegesis (or interpretation) to apply verses referring to general tribulation to the period of time known as the Tribulation or Great Tribulation. This is true whether the passages involve the disciples of the Lord, as recorded in the gospels (John 16:33), or Christians, as recorded in Paul's epistles (above).

Just because believers have always gone through tribulation does not mean the Bible teaches that Christ's church will be going through the time designated as the Tribulation. I have always taught that we need to *plan* as though the Rapture may not take place in our lifetime and *live* as though it will happen tomorrow. We need to quit looking down and start looking up. We need to let optimism replace pessimism. Don't despair for the future, but rather prepare for it; because the Rapture comes long before Armageddon, Christ comes before the Antichrist, the Son of God comes before the son of perdition, the True Prophet comes before the False Prophet, the Prince of Peace comes before the prince of Persia, the I AM comes before the "I want to be," the Blessed Hope comes before lost hope, and the Beginning comes before the end. Dear Christian, prepare for a future that no one can anticipate or conceive.

The Pre-Tribulational Rapture Prophesied in the General Epistles

by David Schnittger

In this chapter, we will be exploring what the general epistles say about the Rapture. The general epistles are James, 1 & 2 Peter, 1, 2 & 3 John, and Jude. A common feature of the general epistles is the lack of any indication that they were written to a single congregation, although in this respect 2 and 3 John are exceptions to the rule. That is why these are known as the "general epistles."

This chapter will explore and discuss each reference to the coming of Christ. There are no references to the Tribulation in the general epistles, so there is no specific verse in these epistles that reference the Rapture in relation to the Tribulation. We will, in particular, focus on 2 Peter 3, as this chapter gives us insight as to the prevalent attitude toward the Lord's coming in the last days, clues as to the timing of the Lord's coming, and the reason for the apparent delay in the Lord's coming.

The Perspective of James

We begin our survey in the book of James. This book, purportedly written by a brother of Jesus, is a book of great practical value, dealing with such subjects as trials (1:2–18); true religion (1:19–27); the danger of showing partiality (2:1–13); faith and works (2:14–26); the problem of the tongue (3:1–12); heavenly wisdom (3:13–18); the evil of worldliness (4:1–10); the sin of judging others (4:11–12); self-will versus God's will (4:13–17); warning to unrighteous men of wealth (5:1–6); admonition to patience in view of the Lord's return (5:7–11); prohibition of oaths (5:12); healing through prayer (5:13–18); and restoration of an erring brother (5:19–20).

From start to finish, James accentuates the practical outworking of what he calls "true religion" (1:27). Despite the practical nature of the book and its authoritative tone, there is little in the way of Christian doctrine. For example, there is no teaching on redemption through the death and resurrection of Christ or the means of salvation. For these kinds of reasons, the canonicity of James has been questioned by some in church history. For example, Martin Luther gave James a secondary position in the canon and labeled it "a right strawy epistle." He did so because he thought James' teaching on justification by faith and works (2:14–26) was out of agreement with Paul's teaching on justification by faith alone. That, however, is a subject for another day.

Thus, as you would expect, there is no definitive teaching regarding the Rapture or the Tribulation in the Book of James. In fact, there are only two verses that refer to the coming of the Lord. James 5:7–8 states: "Be patient therefore, brethren, unto the coming of the Lord. Behold, the husbandman waiteth for the precious fruit of the earth, and hath long patience for it, until he receive the early and latter rain. Be ye also patient; stablish your hearts: for the coming of the Lord draweth nigh."

The context of these verses has to do with the corruptions of the rich, who have cheated and oppressed their laborers (5:1–6). James is addressing these oppressed laborers to have patience unto the coming of the Lord. James uses the example of farmers who wait patiently for the necessary rains to bring in the crop. The implication of these verses is that when the Lord comes, He will balance the scales of justice, judging the wealthy oppressors and rewarding the long-suffering laborers. Notice that James did not tell these oppressed laborers that they would have to endure the horrors of the Tribulation before the Lord's coming.

For believers today, the comfort is that, though we will experience injustice in this life from oppressors of many kinds, at the Lord's return He will balance the scales of justice and reward us for our long-suffering labors and patience.

The Perspective of Peter

As we move to Peter's epistles, the number of references to the Lord's return increases. These two epistles contain more in the way of doctrine than James, and these books were more readily accepted by the early church. The church father Eusebius placed it among the undisputed books. Apparently it was unchallenged in the early church. No contrary tradition is known to have competed with the understanding that it emanated from the Apostle Peter.

It is apparent that the major theme of 1 and 2 Peter is suffering as a Christian and how to bear it triumphantly. It is in the context of that suffering that most verses pertaining to the coming of Christ appear. This is certainly true of the first reference in 1 Peter 1:7: "That the trial of your faith, being much more precious than of gold that perisheth, though it be tried with fire, might be found unto praise and honour and glory at the appearing of Jesus Christ" (1 Peter 1:7).

Here Peter compares faith's trials with gold and finds this tested faith to be more precious than gold because of its enduring nature.

Gold, not faith, is presently valued by men. But God will set His stamp of approval on *faith that has been tested* and will show this approval when Christ is revealed. Then the believer will openly share in the praise, glory, and honor of God.

Another reference to the appearing of Christ is found in 1 Peter 1:10–11: "Of which salvation the prophets have enquired and searched diligently, who prophesied of the grace that should come unto you: Searching what, or what manner of time the Spirit of Christ which was in them did signify, when it testified beforehand the sufferings of Christ, and the glory that should follow."

This is a very interesting passage! It reveals the two mountaintops of prophecy concerning the work of Christ. The first mountaintop has to do with the *sufferings* of Christ at His first coming. The second mountaintop has to do with the *glory* of Christ at His second coming. In the Old Testament, sometimes these two mountaintops seem to coincide.

As a Virginia native, I can relate to that. When my wife and I used to vacation in the Shenandoah Valley, upon our approach from the Washington D.C. area we would see the mountains in the Shenandoah National Forest and the mountains in the George Washington National Forest seemingly all blended together. However, as we passed the first set of mountains we would observe a vast distance separating it from the second range of mountains.

So it is with the two comings of Christ. For example, in Isaiah 61:1–2 we read: "The Spirit of the Lord GOD is upon me; because the LORD hath anointed me to preach good tidings unto the meek; he hath sent me to bind up the brokenhearted, to proclaim liberty to the captives, and the opening of the prison to them that are bound; To proclaim the acceptable year of the LORD, *and the day of vengeance of our God;* to comfort all that mourn."

Notice that Isaiah brings together the two comings of the Lord in this passage. It is very interesting that when Christ quoted from this passage in Luke 4:19–20, He ended the quote with, "To preach the acceptable year of the Lord. And he closed the book. . . ." Later in this passage Jesus said, ". . . This day is this scripture fulfilled in your ears" (Luke 4:21). Jesus very carefully bifurcated Isaiah's prophecy, being careful to quote only that which pertained to His first coming. He did not quote the phrase from Isaiah that reads, "and the day of vengeance of our God."

So we have two mountaintops of prophecy concerning the work of Christ: His sufferings and His glory. This passage in 1 Peter 1:11–12 tell us that the prophets have inquired and searched diligently concerning the time frame that separates the sufferings of Christ and the glory that should follow. Even the angels themselves desire to look into these matters (vs. 12). This should encourage us to likewise search diligently for the signs of the times that signal His coming again in glory!

One reason why His coming should be of great interest to us as believers is revealed in 1 Peter 1:13: "Wherefore gird up the loins of your mind, be sober, and hope to the end for the grace that is to be brought unto you at the revelation of Jesus Christ." The emphasis of this verse is on putting one's hope fully in the eschatological consummation of the grace of God in Jesus Christ. At the present time, we enjoy only a beginning of that grace. For Christians, the consummation of this grace occurs at the unveiling of Jesus the Messiah at the Rapture.

Not only will Christ's return be a source of the fullness of grace, but it will also be a source of gladness and exceeding joy. We read in 1 Peter 4:13: "But rejoice, inasmuch as ye are partakers of Christ's sufferings; that, when his glory shall be revealed, ye may be glad also with exceeding joy." For the Christian who is experiencing suffering and persecution, the prospect of Christ's coming is indeed a source of gladness and exceeding joy!

The prospect of Christ's coming should also be an encouragement to faithful elders who seek to be examples to the flock. We read in 1 Peter 5:2–4: "Feed the flock of God which is among you, taking the oversight thereof, not by constraint, but willingly; not for filthy lucre, but of a ready mind; Neither as being lords over God's heritage, but being ensamples to the flock. And when the chief Shepherd shall appear, ye shall receive a crown of glory that fadeth not away." This word "appear" in the Greek is from *phaneroo*, "to manifest." The faithful undershepherd finds his reward not in filthy lucre or in the selfish satisfactions of lording it over the flock, but in the crown of glory personally delivered by the Lord at His manifestation.

As we move into Peter's second epistle, things really get interesting! Our enquiry is centered in chapter three, whose theme is Christ's coming. Let's take one section at a time, first dealing with those who scoff at His coming, as seen in 2 Peter 3:3–4: "Knowing this first, that there shall come in the last days scoffers, walking after their own lusts, And saying, Where is the promise of his coming? for since the fathers fell asleep, all things continue as they were from the beginning of the creation."

Ironically, one of the signs that we are in the last days is that there will be scoffers who deny that we are in the last days! I believe these scoffers will be in the professing church, as atheists and agnostics have no knowledge or interest in such matters. I know firsthand about Rapture scoffers in the church! At a previous church, where I served as an associate pastor for nine years, the senior pastor had some amillennialist buddies that he snuck on to the elder's board. These men proceeded to make life difficult for those who held to the Blessed Hope of the pre-tribulational Rapture of the church. These amillennial elders derided those who prescribed to what they called the "poof theory" and we were labeled as "Capital D Dispensationalists." All this in a—so-called—pre-millennial church! I also have classmates from the pre-tribulational seminary I attended that are now post-tribbers and amillennialists. These pastors scoff at the idea of the imminent coming of the Lord Jesus Christ to rapture His church. So Peter predicted in the last days there would be Rapture scoffers in the church, and that is certainly true in our day!

Peter goes on to say in 2 Peter 3:8, in the same context: "But, beloved, be not ignorant of this one thing, that one day is with the Lord as a thousand years, and a thousand years as one day." This verse, on the surface, seems hard to understand. However, by considering that the context is the coming of Christ and by comparing scripture with scripture, we may receive a clue as to its meaning.

Let me ask the reader to note Hosea 5:15–6:3:

> I will go and return to my place, till they acknowledge their offence, and seek my face: in their affliction they will seek me early. Come, and let us return unto the LORD: for he hath torn, and he will heal us; he hath smitten, and he will bind us up. After two days will he revive us: in the third day he will raise us up, and we shall live in his sight. Then shall we know, if we follow on to know the LORD: his going forth is prepared as the morning; and he shall come unto us as the rain, as the latter and former rain unto the earth.

The historical context of these verses has to do with a warning to Ephraim and Judah regarding coming judgment via Assyria, and later, Babylon. What this passage teaches is that when the punishment has been inflicted God will accomplish the desired results, which is that the people will admit their guilt and will search out the presence of God. These judgments in Hosea's time, however, witnessed little of such a change of heart. The language would appear, therefore, to reach into the millennium, when a remnant of the Israelites will indeed repent before God and seek His face (cf. Hosea 1:10–11; 2:14–23). Notice the time frame of this revival in verse 2: "After two days will he revive us: in the third day he will raise us up, and we shall live in his sight."

Let's apply these verses to the two comings of Christ. Hosea 5:15 and 6:2 states, "I will go and return to my place. . . . After two days will he revive us: in the third day he will raise us up, and we shall live in his sight." In A.D. 29, Christ ascended up into Heaven (Acts 1:9). If a day is as a thousand years, and after two days (two thousand years) "he will revive us: in the third day he will raise us up," could these verses be giving us a general time frame for the return of our Lord to establish His thousand-year millennial kingdom (the third day)? While we cannot be dogmatic about these issues, it may be that the Word of God has given us a general time frame for Christ's return and the establishment of His kingdom.

Christ has gone back to Heaven after His suffering. He has been in Heaven now for almost two thousand years (two days). At the end of those two days, He will come again in glory to establish His thousand-year kingdom on earth (the third day). While we cannot be dogmatic about these matters, it is certainly worth considering!

Peter goes on in 2 Peter 3:9 to give the reason why the Lord is tarrying: "The Lord is not slack concerning his promise, as some men count slackness; but is longsuffering to us-ward, not willing that any should perish, but that all should come to repentance." The promise in verse 9 refers back to "the promise of his coming" in verse 4. What this verse is saying is that the reason the Rapture has not yet taken place is because Christ is longsuffering and desires that all should come to repentance. If we truly long for the Lord's appearing, we should be busy about the business of winning souls for Christ!

The Perspective of John

As we move into John's epistles, we see references to His appearing in John's first epistle. In 1 John 2:28 we read, "And now, little children, abide in him; that, when he shall appear, we may have confidence, and not be ashamed before him at his coming." Though not directly stated, it is implied here that Christ's appearing may be at any time, and that we should be living continually in such a manner so that we will not be ashamed when He comes.

We find another reference to the purifying effect of the prospect of Christ's appearance in 1 John 3:2–3: "Beloved, now are we the sons of God, and it doth not yet appear what we shall be: but we know that, when he shall appear, we shall be like him; for we shall see him as he is. And every man that hath this hope in him purifieth himself, even as he is pure." Again, while John does not lay out a timetable for Christ's appearing, it is implied that this coming could be at any time, not at the end of a seven-year period of Tribulation. Because of the prospect of the imminent coming of Christ, we are told that this hope is to have a purifying effect in the life of the believer.

Summary

The general epistles do not lay out a systematic timetable relative to the Rapture and the Tribulation. The Tribulation itself is not mentioned in the general epistles. The purpose of these epistles is not primarily doctrinal in nature, but deals rather with the practicalities of Christian living. However, whenever we do read about the appearing of Christ, it is consistent with the understanding that the Rapture of the church will occur at any moment, certainly before the onset of the Tribulation.

The coming of Christ is used as an incentive for patience amidst injustice in the book of James (5:7–8). In 1 Peter, the coming of Christ is to be an encouragement to believers when they experience trials (1:7). The timing of the second coming of Christ is the subject not only of modern inquiry, but it was the subject of inquiry by the Old Testament prophets (1 Peter 1:11) as well as angels (1 Peter 1:12). The prospect of the imminent appearance of Christ is also used as a source of hope (1 Peter 1:13) and joy (1 Peter 4:13) for these trial-laden believers.

In 2 Peter, Rapture scoffers are given as a sign of the last days (2 Peter 3:4), and we are given some indication as to a possible broad time frame for the Rapture, after roughly two thousand years from Christ's ascension into Heaven (2 Peter 3:8; Hosea 5:15–6:3). We are also told that the Lord tarries in His appearing because of His longsuffering desire to see all come to repentance (2 Peter 3:9).

Finally, we are told in 1 John that we are always to be ready for His appearing, so that we will not be ashamed when He comes. Instead, the prospect of Christ's return for the church, and our transformation into His likeness, is to serve as a purifying hope for the believer.

If Christ's coming for the Christian is to be preceded by seven years of unprecedented tribulations, why should we be rejoicing and looking for His coming? This fact that we are to be eagerly anticipating His coming assumes and emphasizes the pre-tribulation Rapture, not seven years of famine, persecution, and death before the Rapture.

The teachings of the general epistles, therefore, are consistent with the doctrine of the pre-tribulational Rapture of the church, and this doctrine is employed in these epistles to bring encouragement, joy, and a purifying hope to believers, not only in the first century, but also in the twenty-first century, as His appearing draws near. "... Even so, come, Lord Jesus" (Revelation 22:20).

The Tribulation Prophesied in the Book of Revelation

by Noah Hutchings

In considering the controversial eschatological question of whether the church will go through the Tribulation or not, Revelation is the most important book, because this book is mainly about the coming Great Tribulation. Therefore, in this chapter we will consider this question in the Book of Revelation, chapter by chapter, to see just who will be in the Great Tribulation, and who will not be in the Tribulation.

Chapter One

The first chapter of Revelation is, of course, an introduction explaining who the human author is, or was, and that the book is about the second coming of Jesus Christ and the signs and events preceding His second coming.

> Behold, he cometh with clouds; and every eye shall see him, and they also which pierced him: and all kindreds of the earth shall wail because of him. Even so, Amen. —Revelation 1:7

This verse indicates that every person in every nation, including Jews, will see Jesus coming. John does not tell us whether the people of all nations, including Israel, will be Christians or non-Christians, the unsaved, or both. If Christians, or the church, are still in the world, we would think there would be shouting for joy. Wailing seems to indicate a negative response. The Greek word for wailing is *kopsovtai* and is associated with the act of cutting one's self in anguish. Therefore, if we can conclude anything in Revelation 1 relative to our question, it would be that the church is not going to be in the Tribulation. Else, why would Christians be wailing?

Chapter Two

When we consider the question of "the church" going through the Tribulation, the church does not necessarily mean Christians or saved. There are all kinds of churches, including Catholic churches and the Mormon church. Therefore, many "church members" are unsaved and will go into the Tribulation. The question should be, Will Christians go through the Tribulation?

Chapter two of Revelation consists of letters to the four churches of West Asia. Some theologians divide the seven churches of Asia referenced in chapters two and three of Revelation according to calendar dates, and others according to doctrine and service. In any event, we suggest there are still types of each church in the world today.

The Church at Ephesus. The church at Ephesus was a church where the members were faithful in attendance and witnessing. The church was careful about whom they invited or admitted into their fellowship. The church hated the Nicolaitanes, meaning those who were gluttonous or immoral in personal conduct. The only negative about the church was putting works ahead of soul-winning, but nothing in the letter to this church referenced the second coming of Christ.

The Church at Smyrna. The church at Smyrna, about fifty miles north of Ephesus, was evidently a faithful church, but probably not as large as the one at Ephesus. The prophetic view of the church given in Revelation 2 is rather narrow. John did prophesy that the membership would suffer tribulation for ten days. However, this warning had nothing related to the Tribulation period at the end of the age.

In the year A.D. 156, the Roman games were held in Smyrna. To amuse and entertain the large crowds at the games, Polycarp was burned at the stake and members of the church at Smyrna were put into the arena with wild beasts. Little is known about the church at Smyrna after the Roman games of A.D. 156. Smyrna seems bitter, and that seems to describe the fate of the Christians of that city. However, nothing in the letter to this church has any reference to the literal return of Jesus Christ, or Christians in the Tribulation.

The Church at Pergamos. Pergamos is about fifty miles north of Smyrna. We have been to Pergamos several times, and the city is practically untouched, with the granite buildings the same as they were in the days of John. Even Alexander the Great passed it by with the comment that he would not waste his army trying to capture that eagle's nest. Pergamos had the best medical facilities of that time, including an extensive mental health section.

From John's letter to this church at Pergamos, it appears the membership was still rather worldly, condoning even sexual promiscuity within the church. In the letter, the membership was warned to put off these worldly sins or the Lord would judge it swiftly. This letter indicates that a judgment of the "two-edged sword" would come. This probably had reference to the short Roman two-edged sword, which did come when the Romans conquered the city. Even so, some of the membership of that church were faithful unto death.

However, like the letters to the churches at Ephesus and Smyrna, there is no reference to the second coming. So the question of the church going through the Tribulation is unanswered.

The Church at Thyatira. The city of Thyatira was an important center of business and trade of the first century A.D. It was also a liberal city for the times, as women also owned and operated business concerns, like Lydia whom Paul won to the Lord and subsequently baptized. The affluent membership of the church were commended for their charity and many good works. However, one problem to the Jewish believers was that the gentile believers continued to eat meat offered to idols. Another problem seemed to be open fornication within the church membership.

According to John's letter to this church, even in the first century Christians were to expect the return of Jesus Christ. Jesus' promise was, ". . . I go to prepare a place for you. And if I go and prepare a place for you, I will come again, and receive you unto myself; that where I am, there ye may be also" (John 14:2–3). The promise of the second coming was an expectation even in that early church (Revelation 2:25). Therefore, the warning of the unsaved and ungodly church members missing the Rapture and going into the Tribulation was a warning, even as it is more so today. The letter to this church again warns that not every church member is a Christian. Dr. Billy Graham has estimated that only about fifteen percent of the church membership is really saved. Certainly, the unsaved church members of the last days will go into the Tribulation period like all unsaved non-church members.

Chapter Three

The Church at Sardis. The church at Sardis, located about forty miles northeast of Ephesus, was a mission of the church at Ephesus. The church was once a very evangelical assembly, but something happened that resulted in a falling away of the membership. The few that remained to support the church evidently became discouraged. The church at Sardis is typical of many of the churches today. The church at Sardis is also typical of most of the church in Europe now, where most members only attend services on Easter and Christmas. Paul warned the church at Thessalonica that Jesus would come as a thief in the night, and the dead church at Sardis was admonished to revive the membership through the promise of the second coming of Jesus.

While the church at Sardis was admonished to watch and prepare for the second coming of Jesus Christ, there is no reference in the letter about Christians in the Tribulation.

The Church at Philadelphia. The church at Philadelphia was a fundamental, evangelical, soul-winning church, which is representative of many churches today. Although most present-day churches are affected by the modernistic, evolutionary, apostate teachings today resulting in a falling away from the faith, there are still some great soul-winning churches like the church at Philadelphia. Evidently, the membership of this church were born-again believers on fire for the Lord. Therefore, John promised that they would be saved from the hour of temptation that would come upon all the world. All the world will be commanded to worship the Antichrist and take his mark and number or be killed. The reference is doubtless to the coming Tribulation period. This is simply another warning that unsaved church members will go through the Tribulation, but true Christians within the churches will not.

The Church at Laodicea. The city of Laodicea is a place of desolation and destruction today as the result of a massive earthquake which crumbled the buildings of this once proud city. About ten miles to the east of Laodicea is Parmukkale, a small rugged mountain bubbling with artesian mineral springs. In visiting Parmukkale, we saw hundreds and perhaps thousands of people there from Asia and Europe, and even the United States, who were there to bathe in the springs for their reputed healing qualities. From the mineral springs, water flows to the west through Laodicea. When it arrives at Laodicea, the water has cooled to a warm temperature, but is still undrinkable. In John's day, what medical professionals there were would make medicines from the mineral waters, including eye salve.

Like the waters in the stream from Parmukkale, the membership of the church was lukewarm—neither hot nor cold. Again, a comparison to most churches today: most church members today go to church as a matter of spiritual insurance and obligation without ever giving a witness or testimony to an unsaved person. The scriptures relating to this church indicate that fellowship and salvation is on an individual basis rather than on a church basis.

While there is no reference in the letter to this church about the coming Tribulation, from the other church letters it can be concluded that the unsaved church members will go through the Tribulation and the saved will be caught up in the Rapture as promised in Revelation 3:21: "To him that overcometh will I grant to sit with me in my throne, even as I also overcame, and am set down with my Father in his throne."

Chapter Four

The fourth chapter of Revelation opens with this phrase: "After this . . . a door was opened in heaven. . . ." Then, John is instructed to come up into Heaven through that door.

John was the apostle that Jesus loved, and he became the early leader of the church as an organization of God. At Ephesus today, streets and sites are still named after him. Jesus gave the care of His mother, Mary, to John, and there is a beautiful retreat area near

Ephesus where it is believed that Mary lived. The trees in the area are white with prayer notes by Catholics.

It should also be noted that after Revelation 3:22, the words "church" and "Christian" do not appear in the Book of Revelation. The obvious conclusion would seem to be that the church has fulfilled its mission and Christians, as promised, have been caught up to Heaven.

The rest of chapter four concerns a heavenly representative scene and there is nothing in this chapter to indicate Christians are still on earth during the Tribulation.

Chapter Five

This chapter is a continuance of the heavenly representative scene as John, who is representative of the church, describes. There is absolutely no reference in this chapter to the church or Christians being in the world.

Chapter Six

Chapter six of Revelation concerns the judgments that will be on earth during the Tribulation, and the number of people who will die as a result of these judgments. However, there is nothing in this chapter about the church or Christians being on earth to suffer these judgments. In fact, Christians are encouraged to look up and pray for the coming of the Lord. If we have to go through seven years of these terrible judgments before the Lord comes, why should Christians be looking and praying for His coming?

Chapter Seven

God never leaves the world and the unsaved without a witness, and this chapter concerns the calling and sealing of the 144,000 Jewish witnesses. If Christians are to be in the world during the Tribulation, why would God call 144,000 Jewish witnesses? The obvious answer would be that there will be no Christians in the world during the Tribulation.

Chapter Eight

Chapter eight foretells the nature of Tribulation judgments that will destroy one-third of all plant and animal life on the earth. But there is nothing in chapter eight that indicates the church or Christians will be on earth at the time.

Chapter Nine

In this chapter, John describes a modern army of 200 million men with modern weapons—airplanes, tanks, atomic bombs—and one-third of the men left on earth will be killed. Maybe President Obama's plan to put women on the front lines will not be successful, as women are not noted. In any event, there is nothing in chapter nine that indicates the church or Christians will be left on earth during the Tribulation.

Chapter Ten

Chapter ten concerns the failure of the nations to repent, even after the judgments during the first half of the Tribulation. Therefore, during the last half of the Tribulation further judgments, as prophesied in the little book (which could be the Book of Daniel) must continue. But there is nothing in chapter ten that indicates the church or Christians will be in the world during the Tribulation.

Chapter Eleven

This chapter concerns the two witnesses of God in Jerusalem that will be killed and then come alive again before the eyes of everyone in the world. Also prophesied is an earthquake in Jerusalem that will kill seven thousand as the judgments of the second and third woes continue. But there is nothing in chapter eleven that mentions the church or Christians being in the world when this happens.

Chapter Twelve

This chapter concerns Satan's hatred and war against Israel during the Tribulation, and the nation of Israel escaping to a place of safety for three and a half years, or the latter part of the Tribulation. Jesus said of this time that the Jews will not have time to even go back into their houses and get a prayer shawl or loaf of bread, and Zechariah prophesied that only one-third of the Jews would escape. The refuge place will, I believe, be Petra, as I bring out in my book *Petra in History and Prophecy*. But there is nothing in chapter twelve that indicates the church or Christians will be in the world when this happens.

Chapter Thirteen

This chapter looks forward to the Tribulation and the rise of the Antichrist and the False Prophet to power over the nations during the Tribulation of seven years. Also, in this chapter there are two references to the Antichrist making war with the saints. This is one scripture that preterists use to try to prove the church, or Christians, will be in the Tribulation.

A saint is a man or woman who has been sanctified, or set apart from others, through faith in Jesus Christ and born again as a new person. The reference is often used to designate saved Jews from those who were still following the Law, or the commandments, for salvation. In Revelation 15:3 these same saints during the Tribulation are the 144,000 saved and sealed Israelites, or other Jews saved during the Tribulation, who will oppose the Antichrist and his efforts to take over the temple. Gentiles were not given the commandments of the Law. Therefore, in chapter thirteen there is no evidence that the church or Christians of the dispensation of God's grace will go into the Tribulation.

Chapter Fourteen

The fourteenth chapter of Revelation presents a preview of what will happen during the last half of the Tribulation, which may be described as the time of Jacob's trouble. The first event that will seem to happen is the translation of the 144,000 saved Jews to allow the Antichrist to have full power over the nations. The second event is to expose the Antichrist for what he is and give the remaining population of the world one last chance to repent and be saved. There is no reference in this chapter to the church or Christians being in the world.

Chapter Fifteen

Chapter fifteen presents the extent of the anger of God against a rebellious world that is now under the rule of Satan's man, Antichrist. Signs and wonders have been given to the nations, and the ministry of the 144,000 saints of Israel has presented the last opportunity for those who would be saved to come to the knowledge of the truth. Seven last judgments are predetermined by God to destroy the last effort by Satan to take over the planet earth. There is no evidence in this chapter that the church, or Christians, will be in the world during these judgments.

Chapter Sixteen

This chapter describes in detail the seven last judgments during the

Great Tribulation. One judgment will be that those who have taken the mark of the Beast, perhaps a computer chip, will develop grievous sores. Some of the last seven judgments could only happen if the judgments are from an extraterrestrial source, perhaps the sun and the moon as indicated. This will doubtless be a time of horror and suffering and death, but there is no evidence in this chapter that the church or Christians will be on the earth when all this occurs.

Chapter Seventeen

Chapter seventeen presents the world government of Antichrist to be of two parts: a one-world religion and a one-world political system—the Antichrist working in concert with the False Prophet. Seemingly, according to the prophecy, the political system destroys the leadership of the religious entity and Mystery Babylon will be destroyed. The Babylon on the Euphrates River of 500 B.C. was destroyed, but during the Tribulation there will be a Mystery Babylon. Some believe it will be Rome where the Catholic headquarters are located; others believe it will be Washington D.C.; and others believe it will be New York City, where the United Nations is headquartered. This judgment may be part of, or the aftermath of, the Battle of Armageddon. Regardless of the course, reason, or objects of this judgment, there is no evidence that the church or Christians will be involved.

Chapter Eighteen

This chapter relates to the aftermath of the destruction of the biblical Mystery Babylon. The Jews are referenced in the Bible as God's earthly people, and John warns according to the revelation he received that God calls out His people to leave before Mystery Babylon is judged and destroyed. Considering this specific part of John's vision, in his time it would have been Rome without question. But today, it could be New York City, because there are more Jews in New York City than there are in Israel. In any event, the reference here is probably to Israel and certainly not to the church or Christians.

Chapters Nineteen Through Twenty-two

In Revelation 19:1, we finally do find Christians: "And after these things I heard a great voice of much people in heaven, saying, Alleluia; Salvation, and glory, and honour, and power, unto the Lord our God."

The balance of Revelation 19–22 concerns the return of Jesus Christ with the Christians who are in their glorified bodies to reign and rule with Him. Also referenced is the binding of Satan and his demise, and the eternity of Jesus Christ and His bride, the true church, in the New Jerusalem, a place He went to prepare for them that love Him: "And if I go and prepare a place for you, I will come again, and receive you unto myself; that where I am, there ye may be also" (John 14:3).

The obvious conclusion is that there will be no Christians in the Tribulation except those who are saved in that time:

> But I would not have you to be ignorant, brethren, concerning them which are asleep, that ye sorrow not, even as others which have no hope. For if we believe that Jesus died and rose again, even so them also which sleep in Jesus will God bring with him. For this we say unto you by the word of the Lord, that we which are alive and remain unto the coming of the Lord shall not prevent them which are asleep. For the Lord himself shall descend from heaven with a shout, with the voice of the archangel, and with the trump of God: and the dead in Christ shall rise first: Then we which are alive

and remain shall be caught up together with them in the clouds, to meet the Lord in the air: and so shall we ever be with the Lord. Wherefore comfort one another with these words.

—1 Thessalonians 4:13-18

The Church After the Rapture

by Kenneth C. Hill

The church is the body and bride of Christ made up of individual saints. Saints are those who have placed their faith in the finished work of Christ on the cross. They believe that Jesus, the Christ—the Son of the Living God—came to this earth to be their sacrifice for their sin. His blood was shed so that they could have freedom from sin and an abundant, eternal life with Christ. They believe that Christ came alive from the dead and ascended into Heaven to prepare a home for each believer. They also believe that Christ Jesus will come back for them, just as He promised.

Those of us who follow Christ are the church. We are the blood-washed and blood-bought saints. We are the ones set apart unto God and from the things of the world system. We are the ones looking for the soon coming of our Lord and Saviour to call us to Himself.

The question under discussion is, What will happen to the church—you, me, and all the saints—after the Rapture? You have already learned about the Rapture, or calling out, of the church. When the great multitude of saints, living and dead, are called out and travel upward—what's next?

We know from Scripture that the event of the Rapture ends the age of the church. The church is no longer on the earth and is not suffering from the effects of the Great Tribulation. That is great to know.

Let's see what Paul wrote about the Rapture event and its effect upon the saints.

He wrote in 1 Thessalonians 4:13–18:

> But I would not have you to be ignorant, brethren, concerning them which are asleep, that ye sorrow not, even as others which have no hope. For if we believe that Jesus died and rose again, even so them also which sleep in Jesus will God bring with him. For this we say unto you by the word of the Lord, that we which are alive and remain unto the coming of the Lord shall not prevent them which are asleep. For the Lord himself shall descend from heaven with a shout, with the voice of the archangel, and with the trump of God: and the dead in Christ shall rise first: Then we which are alive and remain shall be caught up together with them in the clouds, to meet the Lord in the air: and so shall we ever be with the Lord. Wherefore comfort one another with these words.

Paul also wrote in 1 Corinthians 15:51–58:

> Behold, I shew you a mystery; We shall not all sleep, but we shall all be changed, In a moment, in the twinkling of an eye, at the last trump: for the trumpet shall sound, and the dead shall be raised incorruptible, and we shall be changed. For this corruptible must put on incorruption, and this mortal must put on immortality. So when this corruptible shall have put on incorruption, and this mortal shall have put on immortality, then shall be brought to pass the saying that is written, Death is swallowed up in victory. O death, where is thy sting? O grave, where is thy victory? The sting of

death is sin; and the strength of sin is the law. But thanks be to God, which giveth us the victory through our Lord Jesus Christ. Therefore, my beloved brethren, be ye stedfast, unmoveable, always abounding in the work of the Lord, forasmuch as ye know that your labour is not in vain in the Lord.

What do we learn from these passages?

» All saints must all be changed at the Rapture. The resurrected saints and the living saints will each be transformed from mortal corruptible (and corrupted) bodies into those that are eternal and incorruptible. The dead in Christ (resurrected saints) will be changed first and rise first. Don't be disheartened if you are living and will be changed after the dead saints, because it will all happen within an instant. You won't be late!
» All saints will meet Christ in the air.
» All saints (the church) will be with our Lord Jesus Christ for eternity.
» Those of us who read these inspired words of Scripture are to receive comfort in knowing that our Lord is preparing the best for us. We are to take comfort in the fact that our Lord knows our works and that our labor, toil, frets, and tears are not in vain.

What Happens to the Church While the Great Tribulation Is Ravaging the Earth?

The church, having escaped the Great Tribulation, is ushered into the presence of the Lord. While the turmoil and anguish is beyond understanding on the earth, the church will be with Christ!

As Christ told His followers in John 14:1–3: "Let not your heart be troubled: ye believe in God, believe also in me. In my Father's house are many mansions: if it were not so, I would have told you. I go to prepare a place for you. And if I go and prepare a place for you, I will come again, and receive you unto myself; that where I am, there ye may be also."

In His prayer for those who follow Him, Christ's words were recorded in John 17. In verse 24 of that passage, Christ prayed: "Father, I will that they also, whom thou hast given me, be with me where I am; that they may behold my glory, which thou hast given me: for thou lovedst me before the foundation of the world." Christ's request is granted as the church is joined with Him following the Rapture.

In preparation for the marriage ceremony, in Jewish custom the bride would be adorned with jewelry, perfume, etc., for the grand event. In preparation for the Marriage of the Lamb to His bride, the church, there must be a time of such adorning. This is what is often called the judgment seat of Christ or the bema of Christ.

This event is not to determine the eternal state of the individuals who form the church. That was determined long ago when their names were written in the Book of Life at the time they placed their faith in Christ Jesus. This event is to present final recognitions, honors, and crowns to the saints who follow Christ. This will be the time their actions since salvation will be reviewed and each will receive, or not receive, rewards according to their works.

The Apostle Paul writes of this in 1 Corinthians 3:11–15:

> For other foundation can no man lay than that is laid, which is Jesus Christ. Now if any man build upon this foundation gold, silver, precious stones, wood, hay, stubble; Every man's work shall be made manifest: for the day shall declare it, because it shall be revealed by fire; and the fire shall try every man's work of what sort it is. If any man's work abide which he hath built thereupon, he

shall receive a reward. If any man's work shall be burned, he shall suffer loss: but he himself shall be saved; yet so as by fire.

Allow me to say again that this is not a judgment of salvation, but an evaluation of the works of the saint who is already enjoying the blessings of his Saviour. However, that does not make this judgment irrelevant or insignificant.

It is important for you to understand that your every thought and deed will be judged by Christ Himself, the perfect judge. Again we turn to 1 Corinthians for insight:

> Let a man so account of us, as of the ministers of Christ, and stewards of the mysteries of God. Moreover it is required in stewards, that a man be found faithful. But with me it is a very small thing that I should be judged of you, or of man's judgment: yea, I judge not mine own self. For I know nothing by myself; yet am I not hereby justified: but he that judgeth me is the Lord. Therefore judge nothing before the time, until the Lord come, who both will bring to light the hidden things of darkness, and will make manifest the counsels of the hearts: and then shall every man have praise of God. —1 Corinthians 4:1–5

I have sat in the capacity of judge for various contests many times. Each time I have been asked to judge the participants by the rules of the game or other contest. Then I have tried to produce a decision based upon the facts without being partial to any side. It is easy if it is a simple footrace, but may be more difficult in a speech or singing contest. Certainly those that referee basketball, soccer, football, and baseball must have skill as well as wisdom.

Unfortunately, I have known times when human judges, umpires, or referees have failed to render a fair, impartial, and correct decision.

I have watched as it seemed that people allowed their own notions and prejudices to persuade them. That will not be the case at the judgment seat of Christ. He will be fair, impartial, and righteous in His awarding or withholding of rewards. Be circumspect in your dealings, because you will face your actions again in front of the righteous judge.

At the judgment seat of Christ (bema) our Lord will be impartial. Consider these verses:

"And whatsoever ye do, do it heartily, as to the Lord, and not unto men; Knowing that of the Lord ye shall receive the reward of the inheritance: for ye serve the Lord Christ. But he that doeth wrong shall receive for the wrong which he hath done: and there is no respect of persons" (Colossians 3:23–25).

"And if ye call on the Father, who without respect of persons judgeth according to every man's work, pass the time of your sojourning here in fear" (1 Peter 1:17).

Note these words of God's assurance at the end of the Bible: "And, behold, I come quickly; and my reward is with me, to give every man according as his work shall be" (Revelation 22:12)

To which the Apostle John, and hopefully each one who believes, responds: "Even so, come, Lord Jesus" (Revelation 22:20)!

John Whitcomb writes:

> . . . Thus, God intends the bema confrontation to motivate each and every believer—not just church leaders—to serve Him in spirit and in truth. It is not designed to be a horrible threat that produces depression and fear, but, rather, an encouragement to love and serve and obey Him from the heart. In this light, may we, as Christians, be more concerned than ever before about our testimony for the Savior who loves us with infinite love, and paid the ultimate price for our redemption and future glorification.

The idea of rewards dispensing, or bema (translated "judgment seat of Christ"), was a common notion to the early Christians. Dr. Lehman Strauss writes:

> In the large Olympic arenas, there was an elevated seat on which the judge of the contest sat. After the contests were over, the successful competitors would assemble before the bema to receive their rewards or crowns. The bema was not a judicial bench where someone was condemned; it was a reward seat. Likewise, the Judgment Seat of Christ is not a judicial bench. . . . The Christian life is a race and the divine umpire is watching every contestant. After the Church has run her course, He will gather every member before the bema for the purpose of examining each one and giving the proper award to each.

Remember Hebrews 12:1: "Wherefore seeing we also are compassed about with so great a cloud of witnesses, let us lay aside every weight, and the sin which doth so easily beset us, and let us run with patience the race that is set before us." Also think of Paul's writing in 2 Timothy 4:7–8: "I have fought a good fight, I have finished my course, I have kept the faith: Henceforth there is laid up for me a crown of righteousness, which the Lord, the righteous judge, shall give me at that day: and not to me only, but unto all them also that love his appearing."

J. Dwight Pentecost writes that the judgment seat of Christ or bema

> . . . takes place immediately following the translation of the church out of this earth's sphere. There are several considerations that support this. (1) In the first place, according to Luke 14:14 reward is associated with the resurrection. Since, according to 1

Thessalonians 4:13–17, the resurrection is an integral part of the translation, reward must be a part of that program. (2) When the Lord returns to the earth with his bride to reign, the bride is seen to be already rewarded. This is observed in Revelation 19:8, where it must be observed that the "righteousness of the Saints" is plural and can not refer to the imputed righteousness of Christ, which is the believer's portion, but the righteousness which have survived examination and have been the basis of reward. (3) In 1 Corinthians 4:5; 2 Timothy 4:8; and Revelation 22:12 the reward is associated with "that day," that is, the day in which He comes for His own. Thus, it must be observed that the rewarding of the church must take place between the rapture and the return of Christ to the earth.

Harold L. Willmington wrote:

The results of the Judgment Seat of Christ:
1. **Some will receive rewards.**
"If any man's work abide which he hath built thereupon, he shall receive a reward first" (1 Corinthians 3:14).
The Bible mentions at least five rewards. . . . The rewards include:
    a. The incorruptible crown—given to those who master the old nature (1 Corinthians 9:25–27)
    b. The crown of rejoicing—given to soul-winners (Proverbs 11:30; Daniel 12:3; 1 Thessalonians 2:19–20)
    c. The crown of life—given to those who successfully endure temptation (James 1:2–3; Revelation 2:10)
    d. The crown of righteousness—given to those who especially love the doctrine of the rapture (2 Timothy 4:8)
    e. The crown of glory—given to faithful preachers and teachers (Acts 20:26–28; 2 Timothy 4:1–2; 1 Peter 5:2–4)

It has been suggested that these "crowns" will actually be talents and abilities with which to glorify Christ. Thus, the greater reward the greater the ability . . .

2. **Some will suffer loss.**

"If any man's work should be burned, he should suffer loss . . ." (1 Corinthians 3:15).

. . . The point of all these teachings is simply this: at the bema judgment the carnal Christian will suffer the loss of many past achievements, even as Paul did, but with one important exception—Paul was richly compensated, since he suffered his loss to win Christ, while the carnal believer will receive nothing to replace the burned up wood, hay, and stubble. . . .

What Have We Seen Thus Far?

» The church is caught up to meet the Lord Jesus Christ in the air
» The bema or judgment seat of Christ to determine rewards

Is there more that the church will be doing while those on the earth suffer during the Great Tribulation? Of course there is.

After the preparation of the bride (the church) through the bema judgment, the marriage of the King of Kings, the Lamb of God, Christ Jesus to His bride will take place. That will be followed by the second coming of Jesus Christ to the earth and the marriage supper of the Lamb and the thousand-year reign of Christ over all the earth. At the end of the marriage supper and millennial reign, we will see the creation of the new Heaven and a new earth. Just a few momentous things for the church yet to come!

The following is presented in the *King James Study Bible* notes for Revelation 19:6–10:

The marriage of the Lamb: the wife or bride of Christ is the church (cf. Matthew 22:2–14; John 3:29; 2 Corinthians 11:2; Ephesians 5:25–32) and the marriage is the eternal union of the church with Christ following the rapture (cf. 1 Thessalonians 4:17). The fine linen, clean and white, represents the righteousness of the church, which has now been judged and purified at the judgment seat of Christ (cf. 1 Corinthians 3:12–15; 2 Corinthians 5:10). The marriage supper of the Lamb represents the millennial kingdom of Christ, which will take place on earth following the return of Christ (Revelation 20:4; cf. Matthew 25:1–13; Luke 14:15–24). The Jewish marriage consisted of three major elements: (1) the betrothal; (2) the presentation; and (3) the marriage feast (supper). Figuratively, with reference to the church, (1) the betrothal takes place on earth during the church age; (2) the presentation will take place in heaven following the Rapture (cf. v. 7); and (3) the marriage feast will take place on earth following Christ's return with the church (cf. vv. 11–14.)

Called: Those invited to the marriage supper are Israel, who will turn to Christ in faith during the Tribulation (cf. Jeremiah 31:31–34; Zechariah 12:10; 13:9; Romans 11:25–27).

Worship: only God is to be worshiped (cf. Revelation 22:8–9; Acts 10:25–26).

Spirit of prophecy: The person and message of Jesus is the essence of all true prophecy.

J. Vernon McGee wrote of Revelation 19:

Now we come to the thrilling events that concern *us*. In chapter 19 we turn the page to that which marks the drastic change in the tone of Revelation. The destruction of Babylon, the capital of the Beast's kingdom, marked the end of the Great Tribulation. The somber gives way to the song. The transfer is from darkness to light, from the inky blackness of night to a white light, from dreary days of judgment to bright days of blessing. This chapter makes a definite bifurcation in the Book of Revelation and ushers in the greatest event for this earth—the second coming of Christ to the earth to establish His kingdom. It is the bridge between the Great Tribulation and the millennial kingdom that He will establish upon this earth. Great and significant events are recorded here. The two central features are the marriage supper of the lamb and the return of Christ to the earth. One follows the other.

Before you can have a wedding feast, you must first have a wedding. The bride of Christ (the church) is ready, having received her adornments following the bema judgment. McGee wrote this about this magnificent event that is yet to come:

> Revelation 19:7–8: "Let us be glad and rejoice, and give honour to him: for the marriage of the Lamb is come, and his wife hath made herself ready. And to her was granted that she should be arrayed in fine linen, clean and white: for the fine linen is the righteousness of saints."
>
> This will be the most thrilling experience that believers will ever have. The church—that is the body of believers all the way from Pentecost to the rapture—will be presented now to Christ as a bride for a marriage. The marriage takes place in heaven, and this is the heavenly scene throughout.
>
> In Ephesians 5, the apostle Paul speaks about the husband-and-wife relationship when both are believers. By the way, he is speaking of those who are filled with the Spirit and of the relationships that flow from it. You cannot have a Christian home without a

Spirit-filled husband and a Spirit-filled wife. In fact I do not believe you can know what real love is until both marriage partners are believers. Notice Paul's instructions: "Husbands love your wives, even as Christ also loved the church, and gave himself for it; That he might sanctify and cleanse it with the washing of the water by the word. That he might present it to himself a glorious church, not having spot, or wrinkle, any such thing; but that it should be holy and without blemish" (Ephesians 5:25–27). This is the picture of the relationship of Christ and the church. . . .

. . . Ephesians 5:25–27 is a picture of that day when Christ is going to draw us to Himself, cleansed and purified. . . .

"The marriage of the lamb is come." Marriage is a marvelous picture of the joining together of Christ and the church. Notice that the Old Testament saints are not included—only the believers during the church age are included. Even John the Baptist designated himself as only a friend of the bridegroom. He said, "He that hath the bride is the bridegroom . . ." (John 3:29). The bride occupies a unique relationship with Christ. You see, Christ loved the church and gave himself for it. Remember what He said in His High Priestly Prayer: "I in them, and thou in me, that they may be made perfect in one; and that the world may know that thou hast sent me, and hast loved them, as thou hast loved me. Father, I will that they also, whom thou hast given me, be with me where I am; that they may behold my glory, which thou hast given me: for thou lovedst me before the foundation of the world. O righteous Father, the world hath not known thee: but I have known thee, and these have known that thou hast sent me. And I have declared unto them thy name, and will declare *it:* that the love wherewith thou hast loved me may be in them, and I in them" (John 17:23–26).

The thing that is so wonderful is that we are going to *know* Christ—really know him—for the first time.

We read in Revelation 19:9–10: "And he saith unto me, Write, Blessed are they which are called unto the marriage supper of the Lamb. And he saith unto me, These are the true sayings of God. And I fell at his feet to worship him. And he said unto me, See thou do it not: I am thy fellowservant, and of thy brethren that have the testimony of Jesus: worship God: for the testimony of Jesus is the spirit of prophecy."

Continuing with the writing of McGee we read:

> Hear me carefully now: the marriage of the Lamb will take place in heaven, but the marriage *supper* will take place upon the earth. The picture of this is in Matthew 25:1–13 which is the parable of the ten virgins. You see, the virgins were not the bride. Christ has only one bride, and that is the church. The Bridegroom will return to the earth for the marriage supper. He will return not only to judge the earth but to have the marriage supper, which the ten virgins are expecting to attend.
>
> Another picture of the same scene is given in Psalm 45. In this Psalm, Christ is seen coming as King. We are not told who she is, but the queen is there: "Kings' daughters are among my honourable women: upon thy right-hand did stand the queen in gold of Ophir" (Psalm 45:9). I believe this is a symbol or a type of the church.
>
> Guests are present: "And the daughter of Tyre *shall be there* with a gift; *even* the rich among the people shall intreat thy favour" (Psalm 45:12). The marriage supper will take place on the earth. Both Israelites and Gentiles who enter the millennium are the invited guests. The marriage supper is evidently the millennium. You talk about a long supper—this is going to be a long one! At the end of the millennium the church is still seen as the *bride*. Imagine a honeymoon which lasts one thousand years! Yet that is only the

beginning. What joy! What ecstasy! The angel puts God's seal on this scene: "these are the true words of God."

Charles Ryrie shared this insight about the millennium and its reference throughout the Bible: "The millennium is called the kingdom of heaven (Matthew 6:10); the kingdom of God (Luke 19:11); the kingdom of Christ (Revelation 11:15); the regeneration (Matthew 19:28); the times of refreshing (Acts 3:19); and the world to come (Hebrews 2:5)." I suppose we could also call it the time of joy and exultation as we see the benefits of Christ's millennial reign. Remember, the church—those of us who know Christ Jesus as our Saviour—will be with Christ enjoying the marriage supper throughout the millennium!

Noah W. Hutchings has written this about the nature of the millennium:

> As Joel, Isaiah, and other prophets foretold, in the millennium there will be no weapons of war, no national or international conflicts. Satan will be bound so as not to tempt man or nations with greed and lust. However, this does not mean that man will not sin. The excuse, "the devil made me do it," is a poor one. We are told in Isaiah 65:20 that during the kingdom age, a sinner being a hundred years old will be accursed. In other words, during the millennium a sinner will be given one hundred years to repent and obey the Lord. The law will be enforced from Jerusalem, and sinners who continually violate the Law will be cut off. Other than the death of the ungodly sinners, there will be no death during the millennium. As it was before the flood, those in the millennium will live to be almost one thousand years old. We are told that God's people will live to be as old as trees.
>
> Environmental problems will be solved during the millennium, deserts will become productive farmland, and there will be

peace in the animal world—the lamb will lie down with wolves. The curse on nature came because of sin. Adam sinned and nature was cursed. In Noah's day, mankind became exceedingly sinful and nature was cursed again. In these days, there is much concern, and nations hold summit meetings regarding the ecology. The problem is as the Bible declares: the more sinful the human race becomes, the sicker the environment becomes. Paul wrote in Romans 8:18-23 that the whole creation, including birds and animals, are waiting for the completion of the first resurrection when the weight of sin from the ground will be lifted

No man has yet lived to be a thousand years. One day is as a thousand years with God, and the Lord told Adam the day he sinned he would die. The account by John regarding the termination of the thousand-year reign of Jesus Christ encompasses the release of Satan from the bottomless pit for a little season. The Tribulation is referred to in Revelation 6:11 as a little season, so Satan is allowed only a few years at most to do his dirty work. Even after a thousand years of peace, plenty, and perfect government, man fails again for the second time. As the armies of the nations come to destroy Jerusalem and the camp of the saints, fire comes down from Heaven and destroys them all. Whether all the people on earth, not including resurrected saints, are destroyed is not clear. From the account of the judgments of the nations in Matthew 25, it appears that only the goat nations will be annihilated, because the sheep nations are promised eternal life.

During the millennium, according to Ezekiel 40-48, the tribes of Israel will again be divided and inhabit the land given them by God. There will be a huge millennial temple, which according to Zechariah 6, Jesus Christ Himself will build. The waters of the Dead Sea will become alive with fish from the Mediterranean Sea. According to Isaiah 35 and 65, anyone at the age of one hundred will be considered to be a youth and all illnesses, disease, and physical disabilities will be healed. But the lie of Satan is that God is just not giving them everything that they deserve, so when Satan is set free for a few months to test once more the free will of men, the human race makes the wrong choice once more.

Some Bible scholars link Gog and Magog of Revelation 20:8 with the same conspiracy in Ezekiel 38–39, but it cannot be the same event. After the battle of Ezekiel 38, Israel spends seven years cleaning the land. After the battle of Revelation 20:8, the earth is burned up. After the battle of Ezekiel 38, a remnant of the invading army is left. After the battle of Revelation 20:8, none are left. Gog and Magog have a limited number of allies in the battle of Ezekiel 38; in the battle of the Revelation 20:8, Gog and Magog are joined by all nations. The center of Satan's rebellion is located in the race of Gog and Magog; this seems to be the reason for the greatest anti-God conspiracy the world has ever experienced within the Soviet Union of the [past] century.

Will man ever be satisfied with his own estate in life? Not in this present earth and social order. Nevertheless, beyond the millennium lies another chance for mankind to live at peace with himself and with God.

In Revelation 21:2–22:5 we read of the New Jerusalem. One interesting item is that the New Jerusalem is said to be about the size of all the states west of the Mississippi River in the United States of America, measuring its length and width. Is the New Jerusalem Heaven? Is it the final residence of God's redeemed people? Larry Spargimino answers these questions when he writes:

> The answer is yes to both these questions. We usually associate cities with crime, pollution, and traffic. But the New Jerusalem is a

city of unbelievable beauty and peace. In fact, of all the cities in the world, only "Jerusalem" will have a place in eternity.

There are many references to the heavenly Jerusalem even outside of the Book of Revelation. The heavenly Jerusalem has been the goal of all the saints since the earliest of times. Hebrews 11:8–10 reveal that "by faith Abraham . . . looked for a city which hath foundations, whose builder and maker is God." In Galatians 4:25–26 the Apostle Paul speaks of the present earthly Jerusalem and the "Jerusalem which is above."

In Revelation, the New Jerusalem is presented in conjunction with the eternal state. In Revelation 21:1–2 we read "And I saw a new heaven and a new earth: for the first heaven and the first earth were passed away; and there was no more sea. And I John saw the holy city, new Jerusalem, coming down from God out of heaven, prepared as a bride adorned for her husband."

During the millennial reign of Christ on earth the New Jerusalem will be suspended over the earth. It will be the dwelling place of believers throughout all eternity. When the first heaven and the first earth pass away, the New Jerusalem will come down and apparently hang over the earth as a kind of satellite city. The city is a cube measuring fifteen hundred miles wide, fifteen hundred miles long, and fifteen hundred miles high.

In the New Jerusalem there is no curse, sorrow, suffering, or pain. According to Revelation 21:24 people will be able to freely travel between the satellite city and the renewed earth, for the kings of the earth will bring their glory into this heavenly city.

It is possible that the term "New Jerusalem" will have something to do with the destruction of the earthly Jerusalem. While there are references to heavenly Jerusalem throughout the New Testament, the term "New Jerusalem" only appears in the Book of Revelation. Some have suggested that since the Book of Revelation was written after the destruction of the city of Jerusalem by the Romans in A.D. 70, but the concept of a "new" Jerusalem developed in contrast to the loss of the "old" Jerusalem. I rather doubt this explanation, though, since the concept of a New Jerusalem is found in ancient Jewish apocalyptic literature that pre-dates the book of Revelation.

Who will inhabit the New Jerusalem, or Heaven? Noah W. Hutchings answers:

> God the Father, Jesus Christ, and a host of angels, too many to count. We are told the general assembly and church of the firstborn will be in the New Jerusalem. This must be the church of the dispensation of grace, the completed body of Christians which God is called out of the gentile nations. Also the spirits of just men made perfect will be in the New Jerusalem, and these surely are the Old Testament saints. Everyone from Abel to the Tribulation saints who have been included in the first resurrection will be in the New Jerusalem. This does not mean the members of the church will be confined to the New Jerusalem, because from the second chapter of Ephesians it seems evident that Christians will also be involved in ruling over heavenly places throughout the universe.

Remember, we have been looking only for an answer to the question, What happens to the church after the Rapture? We have not been watching the earth through the Great Tribulation with all that happens to the masses. We haven't looked at battles, or catastrophes, or judgments of sinners and sinful nations. We have simply been looking to answer the question about the church after the Rapture. Other chapters of this volume have worked through all those other concerns.

After the Rapture of the church, the preparation of the bride (church) at the judgment seat of Christ (bema), the marriage of the Lamb and His bride, the second coming of the Lord Jesus Christ and the marriage supper of the Lamb, the revelation of the New Jerusalem, the completion of the millennial reign of Christ, we find the church watching the creation of the new heavens and the new earth.

J. Dwight Pentecost gives us these insights:

> After the dissolution of the present heaven and earth at the end of the millennium, God will create a new heaven and a new earth (Isaiah 65:17; Isaiah 66:22; 2 Peter 3:13; Revelation 21:1). By a definite act of creation God calls into being a new heaven and a new earth. As God created the present heavens and earth to be the scene of His theocratic display, so God will create the new heavens and earth to be the scene of the eternal theocratic kingdom of God.
>
> Israel's covenants guarantee the people the land, a national existence, a kingdom, a King, and spiritual blessings in perpetuity. Therefore there must be an eternal earth in which these blessings can be fulfilled. By a translation out of the old earth Israel will be brought into the new earth, there to enjoy forever all that God has promised to them. Then it shall be eternally true, ". . . Behold, the tabernacle of God *is* with men, and he will dwell with them, and they shall be his people, and God himself shall be with them, *and be* their God" (Revelation 21:3). The creation of the new heavens and new earth is the final preparatory act anticipating the eternal kingdom of God. It is now true that God has a kingdom "wherein dwelleth righteousness" (2 Peter 3:13).
>
> In relation to the internal destiny of the church saints, it is to be observed that their destiny primarily is related to a Person rather than a place. While the place looms with importance (John 14:3),

the place is overshadowed by the Person into whose presence the believer is taken.

"And if I go and prepare a place for you, I will come again, and receive you unto myself; that where I am, *there* ye may be also" (John 14:3).

"When Christ, *who is* our life, shall appear, then shall ye also appear with him in glory" (Colossians 3:4).

"For the Lord himself shall descend from heaven with a shout, with the voice of the archangel, and with the trump of God: and the dead in Christ shall rise first: Then we which are alive *and* remain shall be caught up together with them in the clouds, to meet the Lord in the air: and so shall we ever be with the Lord" (1 Thessalonians 4:16–17).

"Beloved, now are we the sons of God, and it doth not yet appear what we shall be: but we know that, when he shall appear, we shall be like him; for we shall see him as he is" (1 John 3:2).

It is the person who is emphasized in all the passages dealing with the glorious expectation of the church rather than the place to which they are taken.

It has already been demonstrated from passages such as Revelation 21:3 that the Lord Jesus Christ will be dwelling with men on the new earth in the eternal kingdom. Since Scripture reveals that the church will be with Christ, it is concluded that the eternal abode of the church will likewise be in the new earth, in that heavenly city, New Jerusalem, that has been especially prepared by God for the saints. Such a relationship would be the answer to the Lord's prayer for those God had given Him: "Father, I will that they also, whom thou hast given me, be with me where I am; that they may behold my glory, which thou hast given me: for thou lovedst me before the foundation of the world" (John 17:24). Since the eternal glory of Christ will be manifested in the eternal kingdom, in his eternal rule, it is natural that the church should be there to behold that glorification of Christ forever.

Here is the summary answer to the question, Where will the church be after the Rapture? After the Rapture, the church will be with Christ Jesus—for ever, and ever, and ever—Amen!

> Bless the Lord, O my soul: and all that is within me, bless his holy name. —Psalms 103:1

The Post-Tribulational World

by Larry Spargimino

Following a long night of bad weather and the rousing wails of tornado sirens, a peaceful morning is a special blessing. So will the peace of the post-tribulational world be a special blessing. It will also be much more than that.

In Revelation 19:11 and following, we read of the return of the Lord Jesus Christ to earth. This is not the Rapture, but Christ's return to establish His kingdom. In Revelation 20:1–3 we read:

> And I saw an angel come down from heaven, having the key of the bottomless pit and a great chain in his hand. And he laid hold on the dragon, that old serpent, which is the Devil, and Satan, and bound him a thousand years, And cast him into the bottomless pit, and shut him up, and set a seal upon him, that he should deceive the nations no more, till the thousand years should be fulfilled: and after that he must be loosed a little season.

The Visible Kingdom Rule of Jesus Christ

The Bible has much to say about God's kingdom. Yet, despite all that is said in the Bible, there are many interpretations of this key concept. Some interpreters see the earthly kingdom presented in the Old Testament as being a Jewish way of understanding the eternal heavenly kingdom. Hence, they allegorize the details of the Old Testament prophets and make those prophecies applicable to the church.

For others, the kingdom is a present reality, with Christ ruling and reigning in the hearts of His children, without there being a future earthly reign or kingdom of greater glory than the present internal rule of Christ.

Still others view the kingdom as synonymous with a visible ecclesiastical organization. The kingdom of God on earth, according to this view, is an ecclesiastical structure, with church courts and church officials exercising alleged "divine right" over even the governments of the world. Augustine, for example, in his church-as-kingdom idea, believed that the church should support the aims of the state, and that the state should support the aims of the church. Augustine recommended that the state compel church attendance and that heretics—those out of fellowship with the doctrines of the church, such as the Donatists of his day—should be subjected to imperial legislation.

On the other hand, those who generally take prophecy in a literal fashion, and who understand the Bible to present a premillennial view of prophecy, view God's kingdom on earth as a complete fulfillment of the ancient covenants and covenant promises that God made long ago. It is particularly the promises in the Abrahamic covenant regarding the land and the seed that are fulfilled in the millennial kingdom. This is the view taken by this author.

Premillennialism certainly has scripture to commend it to Christians, but an added commendation is that premillennialists don't generally try to establish God's kingdom rule on the earth by human force or coercion. The charge that has come about lately, that premillennialists are trying to force a war in the Middle East because of the premillennial view regarding God's promises to Israel, is completely erroneous and ludicrous. Yes, Israel is in God's plans, but the plans have to be fulfilled by God, not by man.

Kingdom Now/Dominion Theology

For some, there is no post-tribulational world because there is no future Tribulation. According to LaHaye and Hindson in *The Popular Encyclopedia of Bible Prophecy* (Harvest House, 2004, p. 320ff):

> The Christian Reconstruction movement began in the 1960s within a conservative branch of Reformed [Presbyterian] theology. Its goal is to reconstruct society in accordance with its understanding of certain New Testament principles and the Mosaic law. The founder of the movement was Rousas John Rushdoony. Prominent contributors include Gary North, Greg Bahnsen, Kenneth L. Gentry, Gary DeMar, and David Chilton. Rushdoony's Chalcedon Foundation has composed "The Creed of Christian Reconstructionism." Listing [Five Point] Calvinism, theonomy, presuppositional apologetics, postmillennialism, and dominion theology as the distinctives of reconstructionism. . . . Reconstructionists appropriate for the church (seen as the new Israel) the material blessings for obedience—and curses for disobedience—originally promised by God to now-defunct Israel.

Others in this dominion camp, though not reformed, are the more popular television evangelists who preach a health/wealth, "name it/ claim it" prosperity theology that focuses on the thought that God's will for you is blessings and good. While this is God's will for His people, "blessings" and "good" are slippery terms that only have validity if they are defined from God's perspective. While every parent wants "blessings" and "good" for their children, these parents certainly don't write their children's term papers or help them pass exams by texting the answers to little Johnny or sweet Mary.

Those in this group believe that if you are having problems, whether financial distress or illness, it is basically because your faith is weak. If your faith improved, your life would improve. The thought is that we are now in the kingdom. Name and claim what is yours by virtue of Christ's victory over sin and death and it is yours.

The Millennium of Revelation 20 —Is Satan Now "Bound"?

"Millennium," meaning a thousand years (*mille*, "thousand" and *annum*, "years") comes from Revelation 20:1–6 where we are told that Satan will be bound for a thousand years. Satan's binding is not punishment or a simple demonstration of God's power over the forces of darkness. The purpose of the binding is that Satan will not be able to deceive the nations any longer (vs. 3). Upon Satan's release at the end of the thousand years, he ". . . shall go out to deceive the nations which are in the four quarters of the earth . . ." (vs. 8). With the current proliferation of media-biased broadcasting and worldwide deception, this is a powerful argument against the amillennial and postmillennial view of things. It is ludicrous to believe that Satan is now bound and no longer sowing the seeds of deception.

Amillennialists and postmillennialists love to claim that the nations of the world are no longer being deceived because the gospel is now being preached worldwide. Gospel broadcasting and satellite TV have made the gospel available to all. Allegedly, this is powerful and convincing proof that we are now living in the millennium. However, several questions are in order.

First, is the true gospel really being preached or is it a doctored "gospel" in the hands of cultists and confused evangelicals? Secondly, we must realize that there is a sharp distinction between the preaching of the gospel and the reception of the gospel. Many are called, but few are chosen. The general call *IS* going out all over the world, but what is the response?

Another problem is the length of the millennium—one thousand years. If there is a "gospel millennium" (the millennium is now), and if we believe in what is called "realized millennialism" (another way of saying we are now in the millennium), the period of one thousand years cannot be taken literally. For those who hold to "realized millennialism," the millennium started sometime in the first century. Two thousand years have already lapsed. How do we fit one thousand years into a two thousand-year period?

No doubt, there are some scriptures that are non-literal, but there has to be a good reason for taking them in a non-literal way. When the plain sense makes good sense, seek no other sense. This is a good principle. The plain sense here makes good sense. The only reason why the plain sense doesn't make good sense to some interpreters is they have a preconceived notion crafted by their policy of reading something into Scripture. This is not *exegesis*—truth taken out of Scripture. Rather it is *eisegesis*—reading one's personal "truth" into Scripture.

It is hard to believe that Satan is bound in any sense at the current time. He is like a roaring lion on the prowl (1 Peter 5:8) and is called "the god" of this world (2 Corinthians 4:4). He has the freedom to put ungodly thoughts in the minds of people (Acts 5:3). But, are there other reasons for taking Revelation 20 and the binding of Satan in a future sense?

In Revelation 20:5 we read: "But the rest of the dead lived not again until the thousand years were finished. This is the first resurrection." It has become increasingly fashionable to regard "the first resurrection" as being a picture of the new birth. Hence, "resurrection" here is not viewed as being a literal physical resurrection, but a spiritual awakening, regeneration, the new birth out of death into life. It's a convenient theory. However, in more than forty New Testament references using the word "resurrection," with the possible exception of Luke 2:34,"resurrection" means a bodily resurrection.

Many would persist in this spiritualizing of "resurrection" by referring to the word "soul" in Revelation 20:4. They say this clinches their argument. "Soul" has to do with a non-corporeal resurrection—". . . and I saw the souls of them that were beheaded . . . and they lived and reigned with Christ a thousand years." However, in response to this, we ought to point out that the word "soul" is used in Scripture to refer to living people—the material plus the immaterial, as in Genesis 2:7: ". . . and man became a living soul" (see also Proverbs 6:30; Isaiah 29:8; Acts 2:41). There is no good scriptural reason why "souls" here cannot mean "people"—John saw "people" come to life.

The reader will also notice that these souls are said to live at the time of the first resurrection. Since souls do not die, they cannot be spoken of as being resurrected. Thus "souls" here refers to the entire individual—a physical resurrection.

God's kingdom rule has taken many forms. Authority had been given to human government long ago (Genesis 9:6). Human government was designed to provide a degree of protection by curbing lawlessness and providing a modicum of justice.

Following the Tribulation (that is, in the post-tribulation world) God's kingdom authority will be more open, public, and clearly evident. Satan will be bound and will no longer deceive the world (Revelation 20:1–6).

With the institution of the Abrahamic covenant, God's kingdom authority took on a promissory nature that can only be fully realized in the future. This covenant made several guarantees that could not have been realized in the present or past. There was the Abrahamic covenant (Genesis 15:18), the Davidic (2 Samuel 7:14ff), the new covenant (Jeremiah 31:31–34), and the Palestinian covenant (Deuteronomy 28–30).

These scriptural emphases are very different from the teaching that says that God gave man dominion and authority over the earth and commissioned man to bring the entire world under the dominion of Christianity, even by force if necessary. The dominionists are wrong. The kingdom won't be on their shoulders, but on *Jesus'* shoulders: "*He* shall be great, and shall be called the Son of the Highest: and the Lord God shall give unto HIM the throne of his father David" (Luke 1:32).

While dominionists talk about subduing the kingdoms of man before Jesus comes back, Zechariah 14 presents another picture. The Lord comes back not at a time when the world is peaceful and converted to Christ, but at a time when the nations have gathered together to destroy Israel and all who believe in the God of Abraham, Isaac, and Jacob. The devastation will be far-reaching, as we see in Zechariah 14:12. The same picture of battle and war is presented in Revelation 19, when the Lord Jesus comes back. He returns at a time of warfare, struggle, signs in the skies, and devastating natural calamities.

Key Passages from Scripture Descriptive of the Post-Tribulational World

Isaiah 2:1–4

In this amazing prophecy Isaiah sees the fulfillment of God's ancient promises to Israel. It is a time when multitudes will come to Jerusalem to learn about the true and the living God. Christ is the judge who will judge between the nations, and shall bring in universal peace with Jerusalem as the world capital.

> The word that Isaiah the son of Amoz saw concerning Judah and Jerusalem. —vs. 1

This word of identification is important because Jerusalem and the areas around it are periodically subjected to terrorist attacks. That will not always be the case.

> And it shall come to pass in the last days, that the mountain of the LORD's house shall be established in the top of the mountains, and shall be exalted above the hills; and all nations shall flow unto it.
> —vs. 2

"The mountain of the Lord's house" is reminiscent of the temple in Jerusalem; but here it shall be "established."

> And many people shall go and say, Come ye, and let us go up to the mountain of the LORD, to the house of the God of Jacob; and he will teach us of his ways, and we will walk in his paths: for out of Zion shall go forth the law, and the word of the LORD from Jerusalem.
> —vs. 3

We notice that the people will give the invitation to worship God. Their hearts have been changed and they desire that God "will teach us of his ways."

> And he shall judge among the nations, and shall rebuke many people: and they shall beat their swords into plowshares, and their spears into pruninghooks: nation shall not lift up sword against nation, neither shall they learn war any more. —vs. 4

We hear much of the "new world order." Here we read of "Messiah's new world order." He will judge and rebuke. The instruments of warfare will be melted down and turned into implements of agriculture. In modern parlance, nukes will be deactivated and missile silos will be used to store food.

Isaiah 11

> But with righteousness shall he judge the poor, and reprove with equity for the meek of the earth: and he shall smite the earth with the rod of his mouth, and with the breath of his lips shall he slay the wicked. —vs. 4

In this present age of unrighteousness there is great injustice, especially for the poor and the meek of the earth.

> The wolf also shall dwell with the lamb, and the leopard shall lie down with the kid; and the calf and the young lion and the fatling together; and a little child shall lead them. —vs. 6

Here there seems to be a return to the order of the original creation where all of the animals were herbivorous (Genesis 1:30). These conditions will be returned to the earth in the kingdom age. "A little child" is totally vulnerable to attack by ferocious beasts, yet in this era a little child has them under his control.

> And the cow and the bear shall feed; their young ones shall lie down together: and the lion shall eat straw like the ox. —vs. 7

Lions are normally carnivorous, but this seems to present a picture when all creatures will be herbivorous.

> And the sucking child shall play on the hole of the asp, and the weaned child shall put his hand on the cockatrice' den. They shall not hurt nor destroy in all my holy mountain: for the earth shall be full of the knowledge of the LORD, as the waters cover the sea.
>
> —vs. 8–9

It is the knowledge of God that brings about the safety and security of those on the earth. Though there is much knowledge of God today, it is imperfect knowledge—knowledge that only presents one side without giving due recognition to all of the truth. It is only when Satan's deceptive activities are terminated (Revelation 20:1–6) that the safety and fulfillment of "they shall *NOT* hurt nor destroy" will be totally understood.

Being filled with the knowledge of the Lord does not mean a mere head knowledge. People everywhere will put God's revealed principles into practice.

It is statements like these that make it hard for the honest interpreter of Scripture to believe that Revelation 20:1–6 could be a reference to this present age.

> And it shall come to pass in that day, that the Lord shall set his hand again the second time to recover the remnant of his people, which shall be left, from Assyria, and from Egypt, and from Pathros, and from Cush, and from Elam, and from Shinar, and from Hamath, and from the islands of the sea.   —vs. 11

The first time was when Israel was set free from Egyptian bondage; the second will be when Israel returns from her worldwide dispersion.

Isaiah 19

> In that day shall five cities in the land of Egypt speak the language

of Canaan, and swear to the LORD of hosts; one shall be called, The
city of destruction. —vs. 18

Merrill F. Unger in *Unger's Commentary on the Old Testament* (AMG, p. 1193), writes: "This passage goes beyond any possible application to postexilic Jewish colonies in Egypt, such as the one discovered at Elephantine. It is prophetic of Egypt's millennial conversion to the true God." Unger goes on to note that "the language of Canaan" is a reference to Hebrew and it portrays "Egypt's initial embracing of Judah's faith." Their swearing "to the Lord of hosts" is covenantal language indicating Egypt's embracing of the faith of Israel. This same language is used of Israel in Deuteronomy 6:13: "Thou shalt fear the LORD thy God, . . . and shalt *swear* by his name."

"The city of destruction" is believed to be a reference to Heliopolis, the Egyptian city meaning "city of the sun." However, since Onias, a Jew under Ptolemy Philometer, built a Jewish temple as an alleged fulfillment of Isaiah's important prophecy, and since it became a rival to the temple in Jerusalem, the name of the city was deliberately changed by outraged Jewish scribes to "city of destruction" (see Unger, p. 1193).

In that day shall there be an altar to the LORD in the midst of the
land of Egypt, and a pillar at the border thereof to the LORD.
—vs. 19

The altar and a pillar will be legal witnesses to the fact that Egypt is now the Lord's land. Pillars were used as boundary markers (see Genesis 31:45).

And it shall be for a sign and for a witness unto the LORD of hosts
in the land of Egypt: for they shall cry unto the LORD because of the

> oppressors, and he shall send them a saviour, and a great one, and he shall deliver them. —vs. 20

During the millennial kingdom—i.e. the post-tribulational world—when God's sovereign authority will be recognized in Egypt, the altar and the pillar will not be primarily for a sacrifice but for "a sign and a witness." Unger makes the case for saying that "the altar and the pillar will become a sign and a witness to the lord of armies of His presence and availability to the Egyptians, for they will cry to the Lord because of oppressors" (Unger, 1193).

> And the LORD shall be known to Egypt, and the Egyptians shall know the LORD in that day, and shall do sacrifice and oblation; yea, they shall vow a vow unto the LORD, and perform it. —vs. 21

This has never happened and speaks about worldwide revival in the days described in Isaiah 2:1–4. Indeed implements of warfare will become implements for agricultural harvest because the old enmity between Jew and Egyptian will be something of the past.

> And the LORD shall smite Egypt: he shall smite and heal it: and they shall return even to the LORD, and he shall be intreated of them, and shall heal them. —vs. 22

It seems natural to ask, Why will the Lord smite Egypt? But the Lord doesn't stop in His activity toward Egypt with smiting: ". . . he shall smite and heal it: and they shall return even to the LORD." God's smiting of Egypt is not to destroy Egypt, as the Lord did with Pharaoh and his armies, but to bring Egypt to a point of humility and then decision.

> In that day shall there be a highway out of Egypt to Assyria, and the Assyrian shall come into Egypt, and the Egyptian into Assyria, and the Egyptians shall serve with the Assyrians. —vs. 23

This highway is not now used for invading armies, but for joint worship and service to God. How different this is from today. Presently, there is great division and hostility in the Arab/Muslim world. The division is not only against the West, and against Christianity, but also there is division between Sunni Muslims and Shi'ite Muslims. However, in the future this division will cease. The road will be open between peoples and nations. There will be no border security, no armed guards, barbed wire fences, machine gun outposts, and bunkers.

> In that day shall Israel be the third with Egypt and with Assyria, even a blessing in the midst of the land. —vs. 24

The point here is that Egypt and Assyria, once mutual enemies and hostile to Israel, will now share in the privileges of the chosen people of God.

> Whom the LORD of hosts shall bless, saying, Blessed be Egypt my people, and Assyria the work of my hands, and Israel mine inheritance. —vs. 25

The words "my people" and "the work of my hands" are terms of endearment and benevolent possession. Truly, in this passage are the words of Isaiah 45:22 seen in their glory: "Look unto me, and be ye saved, all the ends of the earth: for I am God, and there is none else."

Ezekiel 20

> As I live, saith the Lord GOD, surely with a mighty hand, and with a stretched out arm, and with fury poured out, will I rule over you.
> —vs. 33

In this context of redemption, "rule" does not mean an oppressive rule, but rather it means "to show power in delivering the people of Israel from impossible domination." God's rule over His people can be equated with protection and loving discipline. God's theocratic rule over Israel will involve His purging judgments and the exercise of His administrative power.

> And I will cause you to pass under the rod, and I will bring you into the bond of the covenant.
> —vs. 37

This is a judgment that determines who will enter the millennial kingdom. When shepherds counted their sheep, they did so by extending their rods over the sheep as they filed past. Unger's observation is noteworthy: "To save a chosen remnant (Micah 7:14; cf. John 10:27–29), Israel's great Shepherd (Psalm 80:1) will count His own for entrance into the Messianic-Davidic earthly kingdom. By severe chastisements He will constrain His wandering sheep to submit themselves to the covenant to be His people (cf. Exodus 19:5–7), made possible through the New Covenant" (p. 1535).

> And I will purge out from among you the rebels, and them that transgress against me: I will bring them forth out of the country where they sojourn, and they shall not enter into the land of Israel: and ye shall know that I am the LORD.
> —vs. 38

This is the purging that comes on Israel during the Great Tribulation. Zechariah 13:8–9 states: "And it shall come to pass, that in all the land, saith the LORD, two parts therein shall be cut off and die; but the third shall be left therein. And I will bring the third part through the fire, and will refine them as silver is refined, and will try them as gold is tried: they shall call on my name, and I will hear them: I will say, It is my people: and they shall say, The LORD is my God."

Ezekiel 36

> And I will sanctify my great name, which was profaned among the heathen, which ye have profaned in the midst of them; and the heathen shall know that I am the LORD, saith the Lord GOD, when I shall be sanctified in you before their eyes. —vs. 23

Regarding this passage, Keil-Delitzsch observe:

> Because Israel has defiled its land by its sins, God has scattered the people among the heathen; but because they also profaned His name among the heathen, He will exercise forbearance for the sake of His holy name (vers. 16–21), will gather Israel out of the lands, cleanse it from its sins, and sanctify it by the communication of his Spirit, so that it will walk in His ways (vers. 22–28), and will also bless and multiply it, that both the nations around and Israel itself will know that He is the Lord (vers. 29–38) (Vol. IX, p. 106).

> For I will take you from among the heathen, and gather you out of all countries, and will bring you into your own land. —vs. 24

Israel is back in her land again, yet the tiny country is a fortress for fear of further attacks. None of the other attendant events mentioned in this chapter, and elsewhere, have yet taken place.

> Then will I sprinkle clean water upon you, and ye shall be clean: from all your filthiness, and from all your idols, will I cleanse you.
> —vs. 25

This is not speaking about Christian baptism, but is a reference to the Old Testament practice of sprinkling, or washing with water, which was a picture of cleansing from ceremonial defilement (Leviticus 15:21–22; Numbers 19:17–19). But this is more than merely ceremonial, as we see from the following verse.

> A new heart also will I give you, and a new spirit will I put within you: and I will take away the stony heart out of your flesh, and I will give you an heart of flesh.   —vs. 26

The work of the Holy Spirit involves a giving and a taking. A new spirit will be planted within and the old stony heart will be taken away. Israel's millennial blessings involve much more than land, though certainly that is involved.

> And I will put my spirit within you, and cause you to walk in my statutes, and ye shall keep my judgments, and do them.   —vs. 27

The ultimate result of all of this will be obedience: keeping and doing what God requires. While spiritual power is evident, a physical dwelling place is also cited. They will live in God's covenant land.

> And ye shall dwell in the land that I gave to your fathers; and ye shall be my people, and I will be your God.   —vs. 28

This amazing verse shows that preterism and replacement theology are not taught in the Bible. God still has a land for Israel, and the promise will be fulfilled sometime in the future.

> I will also save you from all your uncleannesses: and I will call for the corn, and will increase it, and lay no famine upon you.
> —vs. 29

From these scriptures we see that the post-tribulational world will be a world of special peace and blessing on Israel. Both physical and spiritual elements are cited. Israel will be converted to the Lord and will follow Him in obedience of life, but they will also dwell physically in the land God gave to them.

Lessons for Today from a Study of the Post-Tribulational World

We could look at the future and dream about how wonderful it will be when all sin and evil is put down, and Christ reigns as undisputed King worldwide. But are there any points that we can apply to our lives today that emerge as we study the post-tribulational world?

First: God has not surrendered the planet to Satan. Though wars are raging, cultural values are clashing and the "bad guys" seem to be faring better than the "good guys," this is not a permanent situation.

> And I saw heaven opened, and behold a white horse; and he that sat upon him was called Faithful and True, and in righteousness he doth judge and make war. . . . And out of his mouth goeth a sharp sword, that with it he should smite the nations: and he shall rule them with a rod of iron: and he treadeth the winepress of the

fierceness and wrath of Almighty God. And he hath on his vesture and on his thigh a name written KING OF KINGS, AND LORD OF LORDS. —Revelation 19:11, 15–16

Second: We should not expect conditions on earth to change appreciably until God establishes His kingdom on earth. Every Christian falls short in some way. Not a one of us is living up to the standard that God has set forth. We could be doing better, and we should be doing better. Many of the failures in the world are simply failures in the church. Too many pulpits have been cowardly and haven't addressed "red button" issues for fear that they are too controversial. They may be controversial to the world at large, but for the Christian who is standing on the Word of God there is nothing controversial about them. They need to be boldly and powerfully addressed.

Even with all of this said, however, the changes for the better that can come about through our most prayerful efforts are at best minimal. Though we must work and pray for revival, even if mighty revival comes, this is not the kingdom age. Jesus Christ is indeed ruling and reigning as King in the hearts of His children now (Colossians 1:13), but it is only in the kingdom age that His rule and reign will transform the entire planet.

What then is the responsibility of God's people in today's world? Some would argue that we have no responsibility other than building a bunker and hiding out with our dried fruits and canned soups.

A key verse is Proverbs 14:34: "Righteousness exalteth a nation: but sin is a reproach to any people." To put it in terms of the current situation in America under a left-wing government, there is a correlation between the size of the government and the character of the people. The more corrupt the people, the larger the government will become. Our current (in 2013) federal government is not the cause of our moral bankruptcy, but rather a symptom of it. That's why it's wrong to blame any individual in public office, from the president on down. America voted for those people.

"Righteousness" means doing right because our character is right. Righteous people live responsibly. When there is a loss of character and integrity, however, we don't live responsibly. We spend more than we make and fall into the trap of financial irresponsibility. We need the government to help us out.

When the government assumes responsibility over the lives of its citizens—something that governments are only too ready to do—it begins to control and dominate them. When the government gives things to people, the government begins to dictate how the people are to live. The "nanny state" will always morph into the controlling state.

In both Scripture and America's founding documents the government is supposed to protect, not provide. "For rulers are not a terror to good works, but to the evil . . . for he is the minister of God, a revenger to execute wrath upon him that doeth evil" (Romans 13:3–4).

There will always be some control. Anarchy is never a permanent condition. The real question is, Who does the controlling, and how, and from where does the motivation come? Do people have internal control and restraints, the kind of an internal moral compass that comes through a personal relationship with Jesus Christ? Or, are people controlled by the government through fear, intimidation, and oppression? A loss of character and integrity is always an invitation for the government to take over. This leads to more control, and more control eventually leads to oppression, or the totalitarian state. Truly, "Righteousness exalteth a nation: but sin is a reproach to any people."

Does that mean we should abolish government? No. As Madison said, "If men were angels no government would be necessary." Government is God's idea, but it must be limited government;

otherwise, it becomes Satan's idea. In the absence of personal integrity, however, there are no limits on government. It becomes the monster that it was never intended to be.

Thirdly, we should realize that the consummation of God's purposes on earth involves the land and the people of Israel. The current development of replacement theology, dominion theology, preterism, and eschatological systems that are not some form of premillennialism all have this in common: they are opposed to the consummation of God's purposes on earth. Now, those who are proponents of these systems will deny that, but if they allegorize biblical prophecy and by craft remove Israel from the picture, that is exactly what they are doing.

The kingdom promises and their fulfillments, examined in this chapter, have been explained in some measure of detail for the purpose of helping the reader to understand God's relationship to Israel, and His plans for the planet. Islam will not permanently dominate the planet, and neither will the global government envisioned by new world order proponents. They are backing schemes that are doomed to failure.

All of this answers the oft-raised question: Why does God let bad people get away with murder? The answer: He doesn't. No one is getting away with anything. Justice delayed is not justice denied.

Conclusion

by Noah Hutchings

Upon reading this book, the reader is doubtless of the opinion that the authors believe, according to Scripture, that Christians will not be in the Tribulation. If not, then where are they?

The Christians at Thessalonica were under much persecution and even believed they were in the Tribulation. However, Paul in 1 Thessalonians 2 seems to assure them that only the unsaved will be in the Tribulation period because Christians will be taken up to Heaven before the Tribulation begins. Later Paul comforts them with the promise, "For God hath not appointed us to wrath . . ." (1 Thessalonians 5:9). Christians have always suffered persecution in the world, but the Tribulation will be a time when God pours out His wrath upon a rebellious world. In 2 Thessalonians 2:8–12, Paul indicated that only the unsaved would perish in the Tribulation.

Also, as the authors have presented, Christians are encouraged to joyfully look for the second coming of Jesus Christ. However, if Christians are to go through seven years of death and sorrow before the Lord returns, why would they joyfully look for His coming?

Another reason to believe that Christians will not be in the Tribulation is that the pre-tribulation view encourages the Christians in these last days to work for the salvation of loved ones and friends in order to escape the coming Tribulation.

In any event, we pray this book has helped many to understand the dispensational program and purpose of God that many be saved from this coming seven years of horror. Let us all pray and watch for the coming of the Lord, even today.

We wish to thank all the authors who have contributed to this particular study in that section of eschatology concerning the future status of the church, or Christians, during the seven dreadful years yet to come, the Tribulation. We understand that some of our preterist brethren may take exception with this presentation, but we pray they will at least appraise their own understanding and conclusion about this serious issue. Nevertheless, we leave you with the following words:

> And the Lord make you to increase and abound in love one toward another, and toward all men, even as we do toward you: To the end he may stablish your hearts unblameable in holiness before God, even our Father, at the coming of our Lord Jesus Christ with all his saints. —1 Thessalonians 3:12–13